DEVELOPING GLOBAL LEADERS

DEVELOPING GLOBAL LEADERS

A Guide to Managing Effectively in Unfamiliar Places

Bob Johnson and
Rob Oberwise

palgrave
macmillan

DEVELOPING GLOBAL LEADERS

Copyright © Bob Johnson and Rob Oberwise, 2012.

All rights reserved.

First published in 2012 by
PALGRAVE MACMILLAN®
in the United States—a division of St. Martin's Press LLC,
175 Fifth Avenue, New York, NY 10010.

Where this book is distributed in the UK, Europe and the rest of the world,
this is by Palgrave Macmillan, a division of Macmillan Publishers Limited,
registered in England, company number 785998, of Houndmills,
Basingstoke, Hampshire RG21 6XS.

Palgrave Macmillan is the global academic imprint of the above companies
and has companies and representatives throughout the world.

Palgrave® and Macmillan® are registered trademarks in the United States,
the United Kingdom, Europe and other countries.

ISBN: 978–0–230–33751–0

Library of Congress Cataloging-in-Publication Data

Johnson, Bob.
    Developing global leaders : a guide to managing effectively in unfamiliar
places / Bob Johnson and Rob Oberwise.
        p. cm.
    ISBN 978–0–230–33751–0 (hardback)
        1. Leadership—Developing countries. 2. National characteristics. I.
Oberwise, Rob. II. Title.

HD57.7.R643 2012
658.4'092—dc23   2011047901

A catalogue record of the book is available from the British Library.

Design by Newgen Imaging Systems (P) Ltd., Chennai, India.

First edition: April 2012

10 9 8 7 6 5 4 3 2 1

Printed in the United States of America.

To our families—and to all those from whom we learn every day.

CONTENTS

Introduction

Working in a developing country can be a tremendous challenge and a tremendous opportunity. We know because we've been there and done that. We've both worked extensively in the Middle East and Asia, and there have been times when our experiences have helped us learn and grow like nothing else in our careers, and there have been instances of immense frustration.

We both wish we could have read this book before working in a developing country. While nothing can prepare you for the culture shock and other surprises that come with the territory, this book offers advice that can help you capitalize on opportunities and diminish frustration. The advice runs the gamut, from suggestions about how to handle the range of maturity levels you encounter among employees to dealing with the complexities of saving face. This book will help you navigate the cultural attitudes that impact approaches to deals, relationships between managers and their direct reports, and work styles. Moreover, the advice offered here will give you a sense of your options when traditional Western business practices prove to be ineffective.

This book is not a substitute for learning about your specific country or your specific assignment in that country. Obviously, huge differences exist between Bolivia and Morocco and Thailand and India. Similarly, there are differences between going in as the head of the country office for a Western organization versus starting as a midlevel manager for a company based in that developing country. Therefore, we would urge you to take advantage of any training your organization offers to help you make a good transition and to spend as much time as you can learning about the country and its customs.

We are offering information and advice that is generalized to a certain extent so that it applies across the board—or across the boundaries that separate one developing country from another. We've found that certain principles are relevant in all developing countries. When you're working in a place that is less modern than the United States and European countries, that has an employee population less sophisticated about work methods and business issues, that features a work environment with much greater volatility and ambiguity than the norm, then the factors you face are the same no matter what particular country you work in. More to the point, the advice that is effective in one country with these factors in place is also effective in another.

If you've never worked in a developing country before, though, we want to give you a sense of what to expect via our own early experiences in these environments.

You're Not in Ohio Anymore

Bob's first position in a developing country was running a factory for General Electric in Singapore. He had grown up in a small Ohio town and had spent his working life based in the United States. Shortly after he began working in Singapore, a direct report's wife was having a baby, and he went to the hospital after she gave birth to bring them a gift. Everything seemed fine; the baby was healthy, and Bob said something about how cute the baby was. A look of horror swept over her face, and she protested that the baby was not only ugly but unhealthy. Bob was bewildered by her words, but later he talked to a native of the country who explained that some Chinese people were very superstitious, and one superstition was to talk negatively about a baby for its first month of life, since that is when the devil was known to kidnap only the healthiest, best-looking children.

Not too long after this episode, Bob had a more business-related experience that made it clear that things worked differently in his new country. He was in his factory office early in the afternoon and noticed that the buses were lined up to take people home two hours before the end of the work day. He went down to the factory floor and asked what was happening. The foreman told him that the employees thought a ghost had somehow entered the building, and they were frightened and needed to leave. When he asked how they knew a ghost was there, the foreman said that they had felt an unnaturally cool breeze wafting through the factory, and that was a sure sign of a ghost's presence. Bob asked the foreman what they should do, and he replied that they should send everyone home and then bring in a ghost doctor, who would hold a ceremony in which he would do a lion dance and remove the ghost from the premises. It sounded absurd, but Bob saw the look of real fear in his employees' eyes and hired the ghost doctor. Being a practical Western executive, however, he also instructed his engineers to search for the source of the cool breeze, and they discovered a leak in an air conditioning duct and fixed it.

It wasn't just specific incidents that let us know that working in a developing country wasn't business as usual but also the literally foreign nature of the environment. For Rob, it was working in China for the first time, being picked up in the airport at night and riding in a taxi with its lights turned off so as to avoid blinding the oncoming stream of bike riders and men driving donkey carts. Bob recalls walking down the streets in Singapore with his family for the first time and becoming lost amid the confusing quadrants, smelling the stench of open sewers mixing with the exotic fragrances of Eastern Indian cooking. For both of us it was also going to business meetings and seeing people in kaftans rather than in business suits or having them bow when introduced rather than shake hands.

And then there are the mysterious ways in which business is conducted. For example, George was an executive working for a US pharmaceutical company who was opening an office for the company in Russia. One of his first assignments was to secure office space in a building in Moscow, and he met with an extremely friendly, well-dressed man who spoke perfect English and showed him website photos of a suite of offices in a Moscow high-rise building that looked beautiful. It seemed perfect to George, and when the Russian told George the relative low lease cost, the deal seemed even better than perfect. George told him he had to consult with his superiors but that he was sure they had a deal. Fortunately, George also consulted with a Russian employee of the pharmaceutical company, and when George related what he had been told, his Russian colleague laughed and explained that it was likely that the photos he saw were not of the suite of offices that were actually for rent, and that the lease price would go up because of a series of additional costs that the Russian had failed to mention. He explained that this was not underhanded from a Russian standpoint. George's colleague termed it gamesmanship and said that it was merely a way to open negotiations.

Perhaps the most significant difference, though, is the way a country's history, politics, culture, religion, and other factors all impact every business transaction and relationship. In developing countries, people often have a much looser sense of time than is common in the Western world. They are much less tied to schedules and formal time frames than people in the West. As a result, a deadline may be taken with less seriousness in your new country than back home. If you aren't aware of this fact, however, you may set a deadline and assume everyone will honor it—a bad assumption.

Similarly, in many developing countries, conflicts are handled differently than in the West. Many times, the common conflict resolution practice of sitting people down together in a room and having them hash out their differences doesn't work in developing nations. It's not unusual for conflicts to be rooted in religion, caste, or family feuds. While employees in conflict may be civil toward one another during meetings and other business gatherings, they will be unable to work productively with each other and may even try to sabotage the other person—to the detriment of their teams and companies.

What we're suggesting is that to be a successful leader in a developing country, you need to be attuned to the gestalt of the place. It is different from what you're used to, both in obvious ways as well as in the nuances. We hope to make you aware of the gestalt, or at least help you discover that gestalt, using the approaches we've found to be effective.

Defining Our Terms

Right off the bat, we should acknowledge that "developing country" is a somewhat vague term and subject to debate. For the purposes of this book, we are using the term in the broadest possible sense to include countries such as China, Russia, India, and other places that are far more developed today than they were five or ten years ago or that have pockets of intense development.

There's no question that some companies in these countries have adopted Western business models, theories, and practices and that a growing percentage of their native employees have been educated in the West. Nonetheless, they remain developing countries in the sense that a significant percentage of a company's employees have one foot in the past, some practices and policies in many of these companies are strongly influenced by local culture and traditions, and the country itself exerts a strong influence on how a company does business that is different in crucial ways from how it's done in the West.

Dubai, for instance, is highly Westernized in certain respects. Many employees in companies located there have been educated in the West. Native leaders of these companies are well-versed in the manufacturing, marketing, financial, and other processes used in the West and have implemented some of these processes. At the same time, the country's royal and tribal traditions have a major influence on how business is conducted—being a cousin of the sheikh is far more important in terms of power within an organization than an MBA from Harvard or a successful stint at General Electric. Similarly, deals often get done indirectly rather than directly. In the Middle East, the real negotiation takes place in private while the formal public meetings, where consensus is achieved in the West, are often more for show.

Dubai meets our criteria for developing country, therefore, because:

1. Business is carried out differently—at least in certain areas—than in the West.
2. The country's culture, traditions, religion, and government have a major impact on how people work within a business, something that seems strange or unfamiliar to Western leaders.

Again, these are broad criteria, but even if you're working in a city that seems as modern as any city in the United States, you may find that despite this modernity, biases, rituals, and social norms are rooted in the past and create challenges for you as a manager and leader.

Different, but Not Better or Worse

At this point, we'd like to issue a disclaimer of sorts. You've probably heard cautionary tales or even horror stories about working in a given developing country. Someone told you about terribly outmoded equipment in a manufacturing facility or the corruption that ran rampant in a country and that affected all the businesses within its borders. No doubt, some of these stories are true and can make a given managerial or leadership position more difficult than a similar position might be in the West.

Yet, there are just as many positive stories that offset the negative ones. Both of us have been the beneficiaries of great generosity and learning when working overseas. Colleagues have extended themselves to make us feel welcome and facilitate our managerial work in ways we rarely experienced in the West. More than that, they have taught us the wisdom of patience, loyalty, and flexibility. In fact, just about everyone we interviewed for this book recalled executives in developing countries who inspired them and ways of doing business that they found ingenious and productive.

Because developing countries are still in the process of developing, however, operations, processes, and practices aren't as modern as in the West. Because their customs and beliefs are often older than those in the United States or Europe, you may feel at times that they're years behind the West or that they're burdened by superstitions (for example, the ghost in the factory), outmoded traditions, and biases. While this may be your initial reaction, the longer you're in a developing country, the more you'll appreciate the flip side of their customs and beliefs. You'll discover that some of their traditional approaches may be just as viable—or more viable—than cutting-edge Western practices. Their willingness to take their time before rolling out a program or strategy, for instance, often helps organizations identify and correct problems proactively. In the West, we're often in a rush to get things moving, and you will discover the benefits of taking things more slowly in certain situations.

So our point is that being a manager in a developing country is different, not better or worse than in the West. And in terms of this point, don't assume that things are roughly the same because some or even many of your colleagues were educated in the West. Increasingly, you will find that people in developing countries have gone to school and lived in the West for periods of time, and some of them have attended business schools at Harvard, University of Pennsylvania, and other well-regarded institutions. You may also find that your office is just as modern and the equipment is just as state-of-the-art as in your previous jobs.

Nonetheless, it's likely that major differences remain. Natives of developing countries may have the same education as a Western manager and be as just as bright, but they may not have the same business maturity. In other words, their experiences have not prepared them to work effectively on or run teams, or they have never had to stretch themselves in order to achieve a difficult business objective. This isn't anyone's fault—they simply haven't had the opportunities to work in as many varied business situations as people in the West have. Thus, though they speak the same business language and know their case histories, their experiences have been limited.

What we're advising, therefore, is that you should recognize these and other differences, but that you should not be judgmental about them.

Our Background, Motivation, and Methodology

We'd like to tell you a bit about our work experiences in developing countries and by doing so, give you a sense of why we feel so strongly about this book's subject.

Earlier in Bob's career, he spent a great deal of time in Asia when he worked for General Electric as Managing Director of the Aircraft Engine operation. Later, he traveled extensively to developing countries throughout the world as CEO of AlliedSignal Aerospace and then as CEO of Honeywell Aerospace. But it was as CEO of Dubai Aerospace Enterprises for almost three years that the challenges and opportunities of working in a developing country coalesced for him. He was recruited for the job by one of the most powerful men in the Middle East, Sheikh Mohammed bin Rashid Al Maktoum, with his Dubai Inc. investors and given the charge to build one of the most significant aerospace entities in the Middle East and achieve global recognition. What Bob expected, though, bore little resemblance to what he encountered. Even though he had spent years working in developing countries earlier, that experience had not prepared him for the enormous challenges and frustrations he found in his three years on the job. The influence of royal politics, tribal divisions, financial machinations, and other factors all had a huge impact on his perspective.

Rob has spent a great deal of time developing business strategies for his consulting clients—McDonalds, Intertek, Northwest Airlines, Nielsen, and others—in different parts of the world, including China, Japan, Thailand, Korea, the Philippines, the Ukraine, and Dubai. As an expert in leadership strategy and organizational behavior, Rob consulted for

Bob's company in Dubai, and the experience had a profound effect on him.

In fact, it had a profound effect on both of us. Though we had both experienced the culture shock of adapting to work environments in developing countries before, Dubai crystallized the issue. Neither of us had walked into Dubai cold. We had educated ourselves about the country and the business issues, had spoken to people who had worked there, and had been prepared intellectually for the challenges. We were not prepared, however, for the seemingly illogical decisions and incomprehensible behaviors we encountered. We were not prepared for business practices and environments that were unlike anything we had previously encountered.

After a period of time, we were able to gain some perspective on the Dubai experience, and from our conversations with other leaders and managers who worked in developing countries, we realized an opportunity existed—an opportunity to write a book for people who were transitioning to a leadership or management position in the Middle East, Russia, China, India, and elsewhere. As much as organizations attempt to provide training for employees when they're transferred to offices in these countries, and as much as executives attempt to educate themselves on their own, we knew that these efforts often fell short. It occurred to us that a book providing guiding principles or rules about how to lead and manage effectively in developing countries would be a valuable resource.

In creating this resource, we've drawn on our own experiences as well as those of other executives who have worked throughout the world. Each chapter contains a principle derived from all these experiences that will provide insights and strategies for meeting the challenges you face. Each chapter also contains stories illustrating the principles. Some of these stories are our own, but some are from people we've known or those we've specifically interviewed for this book. In some instances, we've used the real names of the individuals and companies, and in others we've created fictional names (either at the request of the individuals we interviewed or for other reasons).

Ultimately, though, our approach is designed to educate you about what it's like to work and lead in a developing country and to give you ideas and information that will increase the likelihood that you'll be successful in this endeavor.

Four Types of Readers

First and foremost, we're writing for anyone in a leadership or management position who has taken a position in a developing country. You may be signing on to be a country head or CEO or you may be in another senior management slot, but the lessons in this book will be relevant across the managerial spectrum. Similarly, they will be relevant whether you're taking a job with a company that is based in a developing country and working for a boss who is from that country or are employed by a Western organization with an office in a foreign country. While the responsibilities and tasks are different for different positions, the adaptation issues are relatively similar for heads of country offices and for middle managers.

Second, if this is your first position in a developing country, you're probably in greatest need of this book, but we suspect it will also prove useful in your second and even third assignments. It took us a number of rotations through jobs in developing countries before we grasped the principles discussed in these pages, so it may help you even if you have some global experience under your belt.

Third, even if you don't hold a permanent position in a developing country, you will find this information useful. You may be working on a specific project for your Western company in China or Russia that will last only a short time or you may be doing business in a variety of developing countries over a longer period of time. In either case, you're still going to encounter the same issues that someone working there for a longer of period of time has to grapple with, and the book will make your task easier to accomplish.

Fourth, if you work in human resources, executive development, or a related field, this book will provide you with a way to enhance your training process. As we become an increasingly global business community, organizations are ramping up their global executive development programs. Understandably, the emphasis of many of these programs is on the basics—language skills, cultural awareness, and other practical knowledge. The principles in this book provide another layer of understanding beyond the basics. Though we talk directly in the book to readers who need to develop their own capacities as leaders and managers, we believe a savvy training professional could adapt its lessons easily for use in an executive development program.

Why Now?

The obvious answer to this subheading's question is that in an increasingly global business environment managers must be astute about how to deal with people and issues in countries very much unlike what they're used to. This is true whether they transfer to an office in Asia, South America, or Russia, or whether they just have to work there temporarily on a project or task. To accomplish key global initiatives, Western companies need people to hit the ground running in places like China and India. They need to have the savvy to grasp not just what their counterparts in these countries are saying, but what they mean. Companies need people who can get deals done in these countries, who know how to deal with the politics and cultural idiosyncrasies.

By the same token, organizations based in developing countries are eager to bring in Western business minds to help them develop growth strategies, establish alliances with key customers and vendors in the United States and Europe, and implement cutting-edge business techniques. At the same time, companies based in these countries recognize that these Western leaders and managers may face a challenging transition. Thus, they want the type of executive who is sufficiently developed to thrive in an environment that can feel strange and in a business model that operates differently than the Western norm.

Thus, organizations around the world understand the value of these developed global leaders as well as the value of developing other business people as quickly as possible. More so than ever before, all types of companies are searching for individuals who have the savvy for working in developing countries—or have the potential to gain it.

Less obviously, the "why now" question can be answered by pointing to the issues of diversity and leadership. Today's workforce is becoming increasingly diverse. On any given team, it's not unusual to have at least one participant from a developing country. Organizations routinely rotate their people to offices in other countries and rotate in employees from those countries. Many times, too, citizens of developing countries come to the United States or Europe to attend undergraduate or business school and end up being hired by companies in the West.

Along these same lines, Western companies are doing more business with individuals and organizations throughout the world. Even smaller companies may have an office or some other presence in China or India, and e-commerce has brought them customers in every corner of the planet. Similarly, companies no longer limit their suppliers to a select few in their geographic area but scour the globe for the supplier that provides the best combination of quality and cost.

In this environment, it's not just global leaders who are prized but managers who are comfortable and smart about dealing with people from all parts of the globe. Many so-called global leaders should actually be labeled "Western global leaders." These CEOs may speak English, French, and German and have led companies in New York, Paris, and Bonn, but they have scant experience outside of the United States or Europe or Japan. Consequently, they don't quite "get" employees who are Sikhs from India or know how to negotiate with Sunnis from the Middle East.

What we're suggesting, then, is that to be a truly global leader, you need to grasp the rules of working effectively in developing countries, not just in modernized Western ones. The first of these rules involves adapting tried-and-true Western business practices to environments that aren't always hospitable to these practices.

CHAPTER 1

Use Cultural Intelligence to Translate Western Business Principles and Practices

In Western countries, we rely heavily on best practices. From strategic planning to team building to innovation, we subscribe to what's been found to be most effective. Similarly, we hold certain business principles to be inviolable. We believe in driving decision making down to the lowest level or revamping the supply chain processes to operate more efficiently.

These principles and practices are inculcated through our management and leadership training and experiences. From the time we were in business school to our first jobs to what we learned from a mentor or boss, we have come to accept these principles and practices as gospel. We've used them in a variety of work settings, and by and large they have performed as advertised. It stands to reason that we will try to implement them at every opportunity.

The problem is that when we attempt to use them in developing countries, something often gets lost in translation. Standard operating procedure in the West may not translate to a factory floor in Thailand—there, no one is willing to stop the line when a defect is spotted for fear that he will be blamed for the defect. In the same way, the techniques we use to manage conflict and achieve consensus in the United States may fail miserably in a South American country—instead of managing the conflict, we find that our willingness to encourage debate and discussion turns a heated argument into a full-fledged fight.

You can become much more effective in implementing best practices in any developing country. As you'll discover, you can adopt a decision-making process better suited to non-Western cultures; you can facilitate teams through supplemental one-on-one discussions; you can weigh your values against those in your new country and find a position that satisfies both; you can avoid being the stereotypical know-it-all Western leader; you can employ tactics that will help you gain acceptance for your programs and policies; and you can capitalize on the universal desire to make a contribution.

Before discussing each of these implementation approaches, let's look at some specific challenges to implementation, first in Singapore and then in India.

Cultural Imperatives Outweigh
Leader Directives

Earlier in his career Bob was managing director of a large global company's Singapore office. As soon as he started the job, he was faced with a complex production problem involving production mix and priority trade-offs that needed a decision immediately. Bob's direct reports asked him what he wanted to do. Bob had no idea what the right decision was and told his people exactly that. When he asked them what they thought the right course of action was, they were baffled. They insisted that Bob had to set the direction.

He refused. Instead, he said, "Look, you've done the analysis; you've been here a lot longer than me. You're in a far better position than I am to make a decision on this issue."

"But you're supposed to tell us what to do," one of his direct reports, a production director, said.

Bob refused to give in to what they considered correct leadership protocol. Instead, he insisted that they make the choice, and if he agreed with them, he would say so. If he didn't agree with them, he would trust their judgment, and if their solution didn't work out, they would change direction, and no one would be punished for making the wrong choice. "Let's just say that we're making this decision together," Bob said.

Finally, his team reluctantly suggested what they thought should be done in this situation. Bob nodded and agreed with them, and it turned out to be the correct choice.

In Singapore and many other developing countries, the tradition is to defer to leaders without question or comment. Automatic compliance with authority is ingrained in many cultures—especially in tribal cultures and in those with a history of military, religious, or royal rulers. Even though Bob's direct reports in Singapore probably knew that they were better equipped to make the decision than he was, they deferred to their new leader automatically. For them, it was better to let a leader make a wrong decision than to challenge his authority.

It does not help that in many cases Western leaders in these situations are often reluctant to say, "I don't know," especially when starting out in a new position in a foreign country. They want to impress their people with their expertise; they want to project the image of a decisive leader.

A much more effective alternative is to coax a team of direct reports to use their experience and expertise to recommend a course of action. "Coax" is a key word here; if you simply insist without discussion or explanation that the employees choose, you run the risk of alienating your team. They may feel that you're testing them. They may believe that if they make the wrong decision, they will be fired. They may resent the way you, a newcomer to their country, ignore their cultural imperatives and insist they act in ways that make them uncomfortable.

Therefore, ease them into the process of decision making by

- listening,
- questioning,
- encouraging, and
- reassuring.

Here's another story that illustrates how cultural conditioning can impact the decision making of direct reports. In this story, however, the cultural traditions produce a positive rather than a negative result. As you'll see, our point is that leaders must pay attention to how a culture's norms and beliefs impact the behavior of direct reports—whether for good or bad. Jennifer, a British executive, was taking over the management of a manufacturing facility in India for her global corporation, which had just acquired the Indian company that ran this facility. She was working with a group of relatively young Indian engineers, and one of her first assignments on the job was to introduce these engineers to a standard repair protocol that the British company used for a particular piece of equipment. When Jennifer introduced the repair protocol to them, however, they immediately said, "This is not right" and pointed out the things that might go wrong if they followed the protocol.

At first, Jennifer was taken aback by their response; she took umbrage at young engineers challenging a protocol that had been used successfully in many other Western countries. After talking with some of her colleagues who had worked in the Indian facility for a number of years, however, Jennifer came to understand that these engineers had a different mind-set from engineers in Britain and other countries where she had worked. To the Indian engineers, failure was unacceptable, and they saw several possibilities for failure in the repair protocol. In the United States and Britain, for instance, engineers also recognized this repair scheme wasn't perfect but assumed that they could use situational judgment to tweak the protocol so that it functioned effectively as environments changed. But for these Indian engineers, such an approach left too much to chance.

Jennifer forced herself to give these engineers latitude to make changes in the repair protocol. She watched as they reverse-engineered the equipment and created a new repair protocol—one that turned out to be better than the previous one and was eventually adopted as the new protocol not just in India but in the company's facilities throughout the world.

We're not suggesting that you should always give in to your people when you encounter resistance. We are, however, advocating open-mindedness. Their way may not be better than the way you've used for years, but if your people make a good case for a fresh approach, give them a chance to test it. As Jennifer learned, other cultures may have beliefs or ways of working that seem odd at first glance but can turn out to be beneficial. Obviously, you need to evaluate whether a given rejection of standard operating procedures is justified. But even if you aren't positive that your employees are right, give them the benefit of the doubt, especially when you're new to the job. Find a way to let them test their concepts. While it may not result in a spectacular success such as the one achieved by Jennifer's engineers, at the very least you will have demonstrated your open-mindedness as a leader and have encouraged your people to propose ideas that can improve existing procedures and policies. Perfectionist cultures can create situations for Western leaders that are irritating in certain situations—the need for speed may trump the need to get every little detail right, for instance—but they also can help improve quality standards that may be somewhat lax.

Though Jennifer's scenario had a positive outcome, we've also seen such situations turn out quite differently: in some countries people are so afraid of failure that they are unable or unwilling to take even the smallest risk. In Japan, for instance, the traditional notion of hara-kiri (suicide) attaches the severest of negative consequences to failure. While Japan is a modern society where leaders of companies rarely commit suicide these days because of a fall in market share, the notion of major punishment for failure persists in their cultural consciousness. This dovetails with the idea of "saving face"—maintaining a positive personal image at all costs. A loss of face—being humiliated because you insisted on a course of action that proved to be wrong—is seen as much more serious in Japanese culture than in our own. In fact, many developing nations have versions of saving face—for example, in the Middle East. Thus, when Western leaders encourage innovation and reassure people that they want them to take chances and that mistakes made in the process will be tolerated, some audiences don't believe it. They would rather remain mediocre and save face than strive for greatness and risk losing face.

A Foreign Notion of Teams

One of the frustrating aspects of translating Western business practices to foreign soil concerns teamwork. In recent years, the United States and other countries have recognized the value of high-performing teams. Corporations have flattened their structures to capitalize on the speed, creativity, and productivity these teams offer, and they have rewritten the rules for how work gets done to accommodate these teams. They have redefined the role of teams by empowering and diversifying them. More than ever before, teamwork requires skills such as consensus building and conflict resolution.

Yet these team-related skills and practices often clash with cultures in other parts of the world. Equality is an essential core concept of teamwork. Imagine, however, growing up in a country where the government is a dictatorship or a monarchy. In the former, one-person rule is the norm. In the latter, the nobility is inherently more privileged and powerful than commoners. Similarly, if you were raised in a country with a caste system or a tribal society, equality would not be a concept with which you're familiar.

We have witnessed initial team gatherings in India, China, Dubai, Thailand, and Africa where team members refused to contribute their ideas even when team leaders encouraged them to do so. Or, as it happened when one of these teams had a brainstorming session, people reluctantly offered ideas but only safe concepts—ones that were standard practice in their companies and had been endorsed by management. Even when they received repeated reassurances that their opinions are valued and that their participation is necessary if they want to advance their careers, they often remained skeptical (privately, if not publicly). Again, in their cultures, they are accustomed to leaders saying one thing but meaning something else entirely: "We will have free elections," they say, but everyone knows the elections are rigged.

In Dubai, one team we worked with had people from many different countries. While this may seem ideal as far as diversity is concerned, it created a number of problems in terms of the team's functioning. First, centuries-old animosities existed between citizens from certain countries, and it was clear that they had no interest in treating each other with civility. Second, people from different countries had different unwritten rules about how to conduct business. While not all these differences were major ones, all the little things—who should speak first, how budgets should be written, how meetings should be run—added up and created additional tension that hampered effective functioning. Third, people were used to working within a pecking order. In other words, in their countries, people automatically knew how much power each person in a given meeting possessed. In Dubai, people's car license plate numbers reflected their relationship with the sheikh (the lower the number, the stronger the relationship and the greater the power). Thus, people enter a team meeting and immediately know whom they must defer to and who must defer to them.

Yet, most of these people from various countries had one thing in common: they had grown up in barter cultures. As a result, they were used to negotiating in informal, one-on-one exchanges rather than in a highly structured, multiperson setting. At the time, however, Bob was unaware that this was the case. Newly arrived in Dubai, he assumed that the team meeting with his direct staff of VPs—which was convened to hammer out the company's first annual operating budget—would unfold as countless other budget meetings had in the United States. As Bob introduced the budgetary issues, they discussed each item; after a day of intensive discussions, consensus was achieved, and the annual budget was set.

In reality, the team had merely been polite and agreed in principle to the budgetary decisions. Once the participants left the meeting, however, the real negotiations began. In the hallway, individuals began to make deals with one another about the budget that had little to do with what had been decided in the meeting.

In Western cultures, team meetings are the vehicles for getting things done. In many developing cultures, though, meetings are merely starting points. Therefore, don't make the mistake of spending a lot of time in a meeting trying to build consensus and reach a decision. An initial meeting is often a good way to introduce an issue, but people need to have a series of one-on-one private conversations before they will be ready to finalize a decision.

Jeff Johnson, who was the CFO of Toshiba in North America for a number of years, told us about the concept of *nemawashi*, which is a kind of face-saving protocol where you solicit everyone's opinion individually and in advance of a formal meeting so the harmony of the meeting can be preserved. While this decision-making process takes longer than the traditional Western one, it allows a leader to adjust his or her decision and take everyone's ideas and opinions into account before making an official announcement or presentation in a formal meeting. It also prevents the anger and disappointment that sometimes arise in the wake of an ill-considered decision that wasn't vetted in advance of the announcement.

Jeff also explained that there were two types of team meetings. The more common meetings were large presentations, generally informational in tone and highly structured. In these meetings PowerPoint presentations were common, and everyone was exceedingly polite to each other. These meetings were usually attended by a relatively large number of employees and were held frequently—he often had 40 hours of meetings booked per week with 30 people in attendance at each.

However, "decisions were often made in very small meetings (that were held less frequently)," he added. "It might just be myself, the Japanese president of the company, and several other top executives. The character of these meetings was different. The Japanese would let down their guard and talk about their true feelings."

One lesson to take away from all this is that Western leaders need to be more patient when it comes to decision making in developing countries. Many of these countries favor larger meetings that are more show than substance or at least more information-oriented than decision-oriented. The real decisions, though, are made in much smaller meetings of top executives or delivered as fiats by the person in charge. This makes sense when you consider that many developing countries have a history of royal or dictatorial rule, and decision making has always been highly centralized. In some of these countries (such as China and Russia), large governmental groups meet frequently and publicly, debating the issues extensively before passing a law or issuing a policy. Behind the scenes, however, the real decisions are made by the most powerful person in the country or a small, oligarchic committee that meets in secret. Companies in these countries, therefore, often adopt a similar model of decision making, but it may not be a model that a Western executive is familiar or comfortable with.

Values: Ethical Variability

Many organizations are highly values-conscious. For example, Johnson & Johnson is well-known for its "credo," a statement of organizational values that the company expects every employee to become familiar with and abide by. The public relations firm Golin-Harris, part of the Interpublic Group, is all about building and maintaining trust. For years, McDonald's has pounded home the theme of quality, service, cleanliness, and value. These aren't just platitudes—the corporate leaders of these organizations demand that their employees live by these corporate values that define their brands.

In many developing countries, however, people are more pragmatic than values-conscious. Poverty combined with a barter culture changes people's perspectives on ethics. While we believe it's unethical to bribe customers in exchange for their business, this is a common and accepted practice in many parts of the world. While we're quick to condemn this practice, we should consider that in some countries bribery is a way for people to make a living wage and feed their families. From a certain perspective, payoffs to government officials so they speed applications through the system are not that different from the slotting allowances manufacturers pay retailers for shelf space.

We're not justifying bribery and payoffs; we're simply saying that if you expect to do business in certain countries, you had better be aware that this is how things get done. *Baksheesh* is the common term for bribery in Middle Eastern countries; *mordida* is the term used in Spanish-speaking ones. These words don't carry negative connotations for many people there, or at least not to the same extent as in the West.

Most business managers working in developing countries have stories about how their best-laid business plans were subverted by corrupt practices. For instance, Steve was a CEO of a large US corporation that began doing a lot of business in China. On one of his first trips to China, he took the head of a manufacturing operation out to dinner in order to discuss a proposed partnership—the Chinese business executive wanted to form a partnership with Steve's company. As they walked out of the restaurant after a working dinner during which they had hammered out the essential elements of the partnership, the Chinese man handed Steve an envelope. Steve didn't open it then—he assumed it was the contract his company had sent earlier—but when he returned to his hotel room, he was shocked to discover that the envelope was filled with twenty $100 bills. Steve immediately called his prospective partner and informed him that he couldn't accept the cash, that in the United States people can be fired for accepting a bribe, and that he had to pick up the money right away.

Similarly, business executives in the United States may believe that you should trust people to work hard and get the job done, that looking over their shoulders constantly and micromanaging has a negative impact on morale as well as on performance. In some cultures, however, as manager you must be a regular presence in people's work lives. If you don't monitor their work, they'll assume you don't care about what they do. In highly paternalistic cultures, overseers are a fact of life. If an authority figure is absent, people figure that what they're working on is not that important and that no one will mind if they're late with projects or sloppy in their execution.

It's not that employees in developing countries are inherently lazy or corrupt. In fact, many people in India, China, Thailand, and Brazil work much longer hours than their Western counterparts and produce high-quality work (and are paid far less). It's just that work customs in the West may ignore realities of life in other countries and thus unintentionally communicate the wrong message to employees there. In the United States, checking an employee's reports every day may be seen as an insult to the employee; in a developing country, employees may feel insulted if their reports are not checked every day.

Perhaps the most vexing problem is when it becomes clear that to accomplish an important task—or to accomplish it relatively quickly—you have to do something that is unethical or potentially unethical in your native country. For instance, many neophyte managers taking command of an office in a developing country need to obtain a new business license or get government permission for new construction or apply for a waiver of an existing policy. They go through the formal process of filling out forms or following mandated procedures, but nothing happens. They call a government bureaucrat who assures them that everything is proceeding smoothly and they should receive permission for what they have applied for soon, but again nothing happens. Finally, they consult one of their native employees who informs them that an under-the-table payment is expected. They face a dilemma: make the payment and violate their company's principles or not make the payment and fail to achieve their business objective.

While there's no easy answer to this issue, here are some guidelines that generally result in a positive outcome:

- Weigh the values/policies of your company against those of the country you're working in; find out what the legal and ethical practice is for your organization, but keep in mind that it may well differ from the one that's written down or that you have been told about.

- If there's a clash between the two, try to find a middle ground that allows you to get things done without violating core principles. For instance, instead of making under-the-table payments, suggest an above-board action that will provide fair compensation for what you request.
- Be aware that your principles will be tested and that you may face some tough choices. Sometimes if you reject paying a "fee" that strikes you as unfair or illegal, you may have to wait longer than you want to get approval for a license or project. This will be frustrating, but generally you should be able to find a way to avoid unethical acts by developing relationships with people in power, by providing people in that country with jobs, and by paying taxes and legitimate fees.
- When in doubt, use the "newspaper test." When facing a request where you question the ethics involved, ask yourself how you would feel if a prominent publication wrote a story about what you're considering doing. Would you be okay with such a story? Or would you be embarrassed and ashamed to read it?

Finally, recognize that Americans, and sometimes Europeans also, have a tendency to have a holier-than-thou attitude when they first arrive in a developing country. They believe their morality trumps the moral code of other countries. For example, Mark, a vice president for a software firm, began working in a Latin American company where his direct reports routinely took certain government officials to extravagant lunches and dinners, bought them gifts, even set them up with escorts, and invoiced the company for these expenses. In response to Mark's anger about this practice, his people explained that they had been doing this for years, just like other organizations, and that this was a way to ensure that requests to governmental agencies were processed quickly.

At first, Mark was outraged and said that this was not the way their organization did business and that he was going to forbid these "gifts." One of his direct reports, however, explained that the gifts were a good alternative to cash bribes and that they facilitated relationship building. More to the point, Mark's boss let him know that there was no way around these practices and that he would have to accept them. Mark did not accept them for long and left for another job where he wasn't put in such an uncomfortable situation. Our point, though, is that while you should never accept any activity that violates your company's policies or your ethics, you need to recognize that gray areas exist and that what is acceptable behavior in a developing country may not be acceptable in the West. For instance, if in Mark's case his direct reports were merely taking government officials out for lunch in exchange for government approvals and not engaging in the other unethical practices, would this be acceptable?

Be prepared to deal with issues, such as this one, in the ethical gray area, and don't be quick to judge but rather engage in reflection and discussion to figure out what's acceptable to you and your organization.

The Biggest Mistake

The absolute worst thing you can do when posted to a developing nation is to impose business practices without knowledge, humility, and flexibility. Unfortunately, many leaders from industrialized nations enter offices in developing countries and act more authoritatively than they should. The worst-case scenarios involve people acting like the stereotypical ugly Westerner. Leaders acting in this way can be obnoxious in their superior attitudes toward local managers. They dictate policy and often act as if the country where they work is the last place they wanted to be. They don't bother to learn the country's customs or culture. Instead, they reason that their experience has taught them the best ways to market, manufacture, manage, and so on. Rather than attempt to adjust their proven approach from the West to the realities of their new environment, they forge full speed ahead without listening and learning.

This extreme position, however, is increasingly being replaced by the more common moderately bullheaded approach. For example, Angus was a Harvard MBA whose first job after school was at McKinsey; he then joined a Fortune 100 company and quickly moved up the ranks. Senior management felt Angus needed more global experience, especially in their offices in the Far East where they did a lot of business. Though management viewed his one-year assignment in China as a global seasoning process, Angus saw it a bit differently. He sincerely wanted to teach his mostly Chinese direct reports what he had learned in his career about running a meeting, achieving consensus, building a strategy, and so on.

To his credit, Angus went into this assignment prepared. He took a crash course in Mandarin Chinese to help him communicate; he also read a great deal about the country, especially its history and religious practices. He was adroit at demonstrating this knowledge to his people, and the effort he had made seemed to impress at least some of them. Angus was aghast, however, at the overly formal, highly structured way in which meetings were conducted. He believed in free-flowing discussions, in constructive conflict, in being provocative (to stimulate out-of-the-box thinking). Many of Angus's direct reports were bewildered by his approach. In fact, one or two of them privately questioned his sanity—he once brought balloons to a meeting and asked his people to shape them into animals as part of a creativity exercise. Angus recognized that his team wasn't responding to his methods, but he was convinced of their efficacy and his own ability to coach his people into recognizing the value of these methods and using them. His team did not even begin to understand how to participate in this exercise, and Angus soon became as bewildered by their resistance as his people were bewildered by him.

Learning a bit of the language and a bit more of a country's culture and history as Angus did is a great first step, but an equally important second step is to listen long and hard to people's concerns; we'll discuss this topic in depth in the next chapter. For now, though, we want to encourage sensitivity to people's reactions when you introduce business practices. Be direct in asking people questions when they respond negatively or with confusion: What are you having problems with? What would you change to make this practice more effective? The odds are that people in a developing country will have different attitudes about conflict and consensus, for example. In one country people may have a cultural inclination to argue more hotly than would be acceptable in a Western nation; in another country people may consider even a slight rebuke from the leader of a meeting a mark of shame. Once you understand people's sensitivities and concerns, you can adapt your approach accordingly.

Best New Practices

Organizations are well aware that sending an executive to lead a group in a developing country for the first time isn't easy. In most instances, they recognize that they need to provide their people with some training/education to help them make the transition from a modern office in a country they're familiar with to an office where resources may be scarce, where the language and culture are unfamiliar, and where traditional business practices may not be easy to implement.

We've found, however, that the training they provide is usually only a starting point for what must be learned, and that much of the training deals with more general knowledge rather than practical, problem-solving skills. For example, the following questions are often not addressed:

- What do you do when you want problem-solving input and are met with silence or bland comments?
- How do you handle passive-aggressive resistance to a policy that violates your people's cultural norms?
- How do you work toward consensus when you suspect team members don't really agree even though they say they do?

Here are three tactics that we and other veterans of working in developing countries have found to be effective:

- Cultivate an advisor with clout from among the ranks of your native employees.

This person may not be easy to identify at first, since the individual with the most prestigious title may not be the one who possesses the knowledge and power you require. In some developing countries, titles mean next to nothing—the person with clout may have a seemingly lowly title while the person with a prestigious-sounding title may have little sway within the organization. Sometimes, the titles are confusing—"Executive Director of Selling Back-Up and Follow-Up Services" is one title we've encountered (or at least that was how it was translated from Hindi).

So it's best to pay attention to the individual or individuals toward whom others defer. Notice to whom employees look when a problem surfaces or when a decision must be made. Perhaps most important, find out who among your people is considered important because of his familial connections, royal blood, tribal leadership, or relationship to the theocracy or because of some other strength not directly related to business (e.g., being part of a strong network of influencers).

Ideally, you'll find more than one person with clout in your group. If so, look for the individual who exhibits integrity. This may seem like an obvious point, but when you feel like a stranger in a strange land, you may be tempted to reach out toward the first person who seems helpful. Instead, take a bit of time to observe whether someone exhibits strong principles, embraces straight talk, and shows consistency in behavior. Finding someone with clout to help you implement policies and practices is great, but you need to trust this advisor to provide you with the best suggestions (rather than with what's best for him or her).

In Dubai, Bob found an advisor who facilitated the often difficult task of dealing with an enormously diverse team. Bob needed someone who could rise above the game-playing and didn't have the personal agenda that so many people there were pursuing. Abdul was the right person because he had strong connections to the sheikh and had access to his inner circle. He understood how to get things done not only within an organizational context but in the country at large. Abdul also understood business strategy and the particular goals Bob had set. And finally, he could speak other people's language both literally and figuratively. Not only was he skilled at recognizing what other people wanted and needed, but he spoke 24 different languages.

- Differentiate between education and experience in execution.

More than ever before, managers in developing countries have decent and sometimes outstanding educational backgrounds. What they often lack, however, is the practical experience in modern systems that can help them learn and grow. While they may give the appearance of professionalism and advanced thinking in business, they may still work in ways that are counterproductive because they have one foot stuck in the past.

The danger for Western leaders new to these environments is to assume that education is enough. Generally, it's insufficient. Leaders need to monitor their people as they introduce new processes and procedures and see how they take to them. In many instances, leaders must take on the role of coach, providing the one-on-one listening and teaching that can help their people compensate for a lack of experience in implementation.

For instance, Lindsey, a top executive with a large American corporation, was given the opportunity to take on a leadership position in the company's newly opened office in India. When she arrived and met her team, she was pleasantly surprised to find that they were extraordinarily well-educated—the majority had gone to undergraduate or graduate school at Ivy League schools or top universities in Britain and other Western countries. They were knowledgeable about most of the business practices she intended to introduce and seemed eager to help her implement them. But when Lindsey began rolling out a new quality improvement program in one of the company's plants, it was a disaster. One of her people insisted on micromanaging every detail of the program, creating morale problems. Another team member encountered resistance from the plant foreman to one aspect of the program, and because this person was married to the foreman's sister, he agreed to allow the foreman to rely on some of the old methods of checking parts for defects rather than adopt the process Lindsey advocated.

- Identify and use the motivation that fits the culture.

While motivation varies by the individual—John works for the money, Jill works for affiliation/inclusion, Joe works to satisfy his need to achieve—it is relatively easy for Western leaders to figure out what will motivate their direct reports. When you come from the same culture as your people, you generally have the background necessary to interpret their behavior and words and figure out what drives them.

This is more difficult to do when your people come from a foreign culture and you're not familiar with the forces that motivate them. In the Middle East and China, for instance, many people are driven by a desire to learn. Unlike in some Western cultures (certain European countries, for example), many people in these two regions are open to new ideas and approaches; they are also open to concepts that didn't originate in their native countries. Thus, they tend to respond positively when you give them the chance to learn about something that strikes them as valuable. By explaining why a given business practice will have value to them and their organizations, you can motivate them to master it.

In some countries, family is the paramount value and matters far more than money, success, camaraderie, and other values. A rising executive in the West may have no problem with a schedule that calls for him to travel two weeks every month. In other countries, though, if you make such a request of an employee, he may refuse or resent that you had the temerity to make such a request. More to the point, you need to find ways to communicate how an employee's family will benefit if he embraces the practices and policies you favor. You might make a case for your approach by explaining how the benefit plans will provide his family with long-term security and that the company provides loans and offers other programs to help kids attend college. If you succeed in communicating honestly how a company can help an employee's family, you are much more likely to convince that employee to try your favored practices—and to do so with energy and commitment.

In some instances, status is the primary motivator. In other words, people in countries with caste systems or other ways of defining status within a society value jobs that can elevate them in the eyes of their fellow citizens. Thus, they are motivated by the chance to shine, to say or do something that raises their status. If you provide opportunities for them to raise their standing within a community, they will work harder and more creatively at the tasks you assign them.

For example, Rob recalls visiting a Toyota plant in Japan and seeing a number of employees sitting around a table discussing various issues. Suddenly, one man stood up and announced, "The sun roof leaks." The people at the table rose as one and applauded, and this man beamed. As it was explained to Rob afterward by other Toyota executives, this individual had gained great status by identifying a fixable problem. The engineering process at the plant was set up to give people the opportunity to gain status in this way, and they responded to the opportunity with great enthusiasm.

Francis Yuen, a former CEO of Trane in China who has also worked extensively in Asia (as the CEO of Hong Leong Asia), was particularly struck by what motivated Chinese business people. He told us that "Typical ambitious Chinese managers feel uneasy if they're not moving up after two or three years. They see so many companies coming in and so many opportunities, they figure that if it doesn't happen at their current company, they can always move somewhere else. The Chinese are very concerned with reward, and they are not shy about asking for compensation."

"To motivate them, you need to really be able to communicate, and do so more frequently [than in the West]. They are always very anxious about what's going to happen. They're looking for advancement all the time. They love companies that can offer them training, so that's motivating.

But just as important, make sure there is a visible career path ahead of them."

Everyone Wants to Make a Contribution

Realize how easy it is to jump to the wrong conclusions when you lack a deep understanding of other people's customs, language, and values. While you may possess a surface understanding because you've talked to people who have worked in a country for years and because you have read about the country—and because you went through a training regimen to prepare you for the assignment—you are missing the in-depth knowledge that will help you read people's responses accurately.

Therefore, if you find yourself reacting angrily to the way your people go about their work or if you're bewildered by how they conduct business, be patient. Give yourself time to learn more about who they are and how they do things— and give them more time to understand what your favored practices are all about.

We've found that the vast majority of people want to contribute to their teams and organizations, even though they may not communicate that desire in a way that a Western leader can grasp at first. If you rely on some of the lessons of this chapter, though, you'll find that you can help people contribute and either adopt your practices or improve upon them.

CHAPTER 2

Learn to Speak Softly . . . and Listen Hard

Most Western leaders go into developing countries and talk a lot and listen a little. They often take an authoritative tone and lecture rather than question. Frustrated by what they perceive as a lack of business understanding and sophistication, they speak loudly and impatiently.

As you might suspect, this is not the way to communicate effectively in these countries. Yet it's understandable. Whether managers are working in Sri Lanka, Mumbai, Shanghai, or Tripoli, they are going to find themselves dealing with language and cultural barriers making clear communication difficult. In addition, they face individuals who don't always speak the same business language. As one executive who worked in a small South American company related, when he asked a direct report to organize a team to work on a project, he emphasized that he wanted a "diverse team in keeping with the company's recent diversity initiative." When this direct report presented him with a list of people for the team, the executive discovered that he had taken the request literally—the list included old and young, tall and short, factory workers and executive staff, natives as well as people from other countries. The problem was that most of them lacked the expertise to fulfill the team's mission (related to a manufacturing improvement). In fact, one proposed member was a custodian in one of the company's factories.

Francis Yuen, the former CEO of Trane who worked extensively in China, told us about another obstacle to open and honest communication. As he put it, "Friendship comes first, before business. They [employees] want to assess you, and they want to see if you're someone they can trust." In other words, if you start making assignments and demanding results right off the bat, you'll have difficulty establishing a productive relationship with your people.

Recalling joint ventures he attempted to set up with his Western employer and Chinese companies, Francis said, "Because of lack of understanding of their culture or background, we go to the table with a different set of expectations. And we thought we had a meeting of minds, but we didn't."

He also remarked on the gap between the mind-set of people in China and that of people in the West: "The customers don't behave the same way as customers in the United States or Europe. And employees—the managers themselves we hire don't think the same way as the folks back in the

United States or Europe. . . . You've got to crack that under-standing of the culture, the customers."

Listening helps unlock the mystery of communicating with people whose perspectives differ from that of employees in the West. Unfortunately, when Western business leaders encounter these situations, they tend to respond in the same way that someone might when speaking to an elderly person who can't hear well—they raise their voice and enunciate every word. Or they talk to their people like they are chil-dren. In either case, their communication is demeaning and ineffective.

What we have learned from our experience and our interviews is that to communicate effectively in develop-ing countries, you have to listen hard, speak softly, simply, and repetitively. In many instances, the action that is most neglected and misunderstood is the "listening hard" part, so let's look at that one first.

The Challenge of Listening

Many managers start out working in a developing country and are eager to hear what others have to say. They are excited about the assignment and the opportunity it represents and want to take in information and ideas. But relatively soon after they arrive, they find themselves unable or unwilling to listen very deeply. For example, Jerry, who was opening offices for a US retailer in Thailand, describes his experience when he arrived in Bangkok:

"It was my first assignment in a place like Thailand, and I really was looking forward to it. When I arrived and was introduced to the people in Bangkok with whom I'd be working, I had a series of conversations with them, and I asked them a million questions. Unfortunately, there was the language problem, and even though I had a translator, the responses were so innocuous or confusing that they were virtually worthless. More than that, though, I was so over-whelmed by the culture and my responsibilities that my sole focus became getting things done. If you've ever been to Bangkok, you know it's one of busiest, noisiest, most humid, and most crowded cities on earth—just dealing with the city was a challenge. So I found myself telling people what to do and not paying attention to much beyond whether they were doing it."

Jerry is describing barriers to listening, and the same ones exist in just about every developing country. To overcome them, it helps to name them, understand them, and make a conscious effort to listen despite them. To that end, here are the four main barriers to listening leaders and managers are likely to face:

Translation Problems

It may be that the people you're trying to listen to don't speak your language and your translator is not doing a good job of explaining what they're telling you. In most instances, however, people who are in white-collar positions speak some English or another Western language and can make themselves understood. The real translation problem, then, is often cultural. We've found that individuals in these coun-tries have different communication styles than we're used to. They may be less direct than we are. Or they may tell a story that's designed to make their point rather than address the issue squarely. Or they may use expressions and refer to people and events you're not familiar with.

As frustrating as these conversations can be, they should motivate managers to listen harder. Listening harder means requesting clarification when you don't grasp the point. It also means being unusually patient—not an easy thing for Western executives who are used to cutting to the chase and favor "long stories short." Sooner or later, executives who listen will "get it," but it may take more time and talking to more people than they're accustomed to.

Reticence

Many times, employees are reluctant to tell Western managers the unvarnished truth. In some cases, they come from cultures where reticence is a survival skill—messengers delivering bad news to leaders are shot (figuratively speaking). In other instances, these cultures suffer from some degree of xenophobia. People are unwilling to be as honest with a Western leader as they would be with one of their own out of fear or anger. It's also possible that these individuals have had negative experiences with Western managers in the past, ones where they told the truth about a business problem and were blamed for it—or thought they were being blamed because of poor communication.

Moreover, some cultures favor slow, indirect communication over fast, direct talk. Reckard Hedeby has been a CEO in Central American countries as well as in Mexico and Eastern Europe, and he has found that in Costa Rica (where he was a CEO) Western leaders need to show greater patience than they normally might.

"We sit down in a meeting [in the West] and we have half an hour to go through a list of things and just jam through them, and we do not worry about people's feelings. In Costa Rica, you can't really do that—that half-hour meeting will probably take two hours. You have to get down into the detail and give people a chance to feel like they're being part of the decision making."

"If you get into a conversation about a specific subject, they're not likely to disagree with you even if they think that you're wrong. So, you need to let people feel comfortable enough so they can challenge the status quo or understand that you want their input. We've had to build that trust over time."

Therefore, if you make an effort to listen but aren't getting much of a response, the first step is to figure out why. If the problem is a cultural issue, you may need to reiterate the importance of open and honest communication; you may need to enlist a respected employee who is native to that country to reinforce that your company's culture is different from their culture, at least in certain respects. Still, it takes time to overcome distrust. Be patient and let people get to know you. When they realize you are not like the manager who "burned" them in the past and that you value their ideas, they will probably start speaking more candidly. Sooner or later, you'll find that some direct reports will open up and provide you with valuable insights—as long as you keep listening.

Being Overwhelmed

This is probably the most insidious barrier since you don't even realize it has become an obstacle to listening. In our earlier example, Jerry described being dazzled and dizzied by the sensory overload of Bangkok. But sometimes, it's not just the location itself but the entire gestalt of living and working in another country that stands in the way of listening.

Gillian, for instance, worked for a large management consulting firm, and she was asked to spend a year at one of her client's locations in Southeast Asia. Gillian, her husband, and their two small children relocated, thinking it would be an adventure. While Gillian found the work itself challenging and rewarding—her client, a Chinese company, wanted her to help their Southeast Asian group restructure and restrategize to operate more profitably. She encountered one problem after another: the house her family was renting was infested with bugs, her husband developed a mysterious illness that lasted for over a month, her children's school was inadequate, and she had to find a new school for them. Where her business was concerned, things were not much better: one of her top people resigned only days after she arrived in the country. A government official began visiting the office regularly asking for "favors"—a job for a cousin, a donation to a local charity—and implied that if Gillian didn't comply with these requests the office might encounter "problems."

Gillian had always been a good listener, and at first she tried to hear what her people were telling her, but within a month of her arrival, she was just trying to keep her head above water. She felt she didn't have time for listening or anything else except addressing whatever crisis was popping up at the moment. Instead of taking the time and making the effort to have good, open-ended exchanges with her team members, Gillian only had conversations with them about business—she was so overwhelmed, she couldn't focus on just listening.

If you're in a similar situation, you obviously need to cope with all the small crises in your personal and professional life. But usually the crisis ends and the feeling of being overwhelmed ebbs (at least for a while). You'll have windows of time in which you have the time and energy to listen, so take advantage of them. Even a little bit of intense listening can go a long way to making you more effective in your job.

Becoming the Answer Person

In some developing countries, the new Western leader takes over a group or an office and people view him or her as a savior. They recognize that his experience and expertise is more extensive than theirs, and they look to him to solve problems and capitalize on opportunities. In some instances, certainly, their esteem of the Western leader is inflated (and that leader may realize they expect too much), but the leader is still cast in a certain role. A number of people we interviewed commented on how they took up their post in a developing country and felt like people looked to them for answers. As a result, they felt they had to live up to people's expectations, and so they rarely asked questions (which would betray their lack of knowledge) and spent most of their time providing answers (not always the right ones) rather than listening.

If you find yourself cast as the Answer Person and this role prevents you from listening fully and consistently to what your people have to say, do the following:

- Impress on your people that your business knowledge will only be of value to them if they share their knowledge of the country and how they do business there.
- Communicate what specifically you need to know from them in order to put your answers into action. For instance, what information do you require about the government regulatory process to get approval for a new factory?

There is a saying, "Ready, aim, fire." This is a good motto for listening. Before making a decision or taking an action, get ready by collecting as much information and as many ideas from your people as possible. Remind yourself that you're out of your depth, at least from a cultural perspective. Before aiming at a target or even considering your options, weigh the input you receive against your business experience and skills. Only then can you pull the trigger and expect to hit the mark. If you do what some Western executives do—fire, ready, aim—then all you're doing is acting first and justifying your action after the fact.

Communication Styles and Substance:
The Impact You Have on Each Other

In general, Western business executives do not realize how what they say and how they say it affects people in a developing country, and they are not prepared to understand the particular communication idiosyncrasies of their employees. Let's focus on your communication approach first.

In the United States and many other developed nations, business leaders recognize that they will be met with a certain amount of skepticism and cynicism when they talk. They understand that their teams will take their words with a grain of salt and not accept everything they say as gospel. For this reason, they don't anticipate their impact when they say something like, "From now on, I'm not going to tolerate people who don't give a hundred percent of their energy and effort to this company." In the West, people would understand that the boss simply wants people to try harder, but in a developing country this statement might cause employees to devote their time and energy to appearing to be busy— rather than working on real issues, they are making a great show of being devoted, dedicated workers.

Therefore, the advice here is simple: Think before you speak. More specifically, consider potential overreactions to what you say and edit yourself in advance to minimize these overreactions. For instance, when Bob first began working in Singapore, he arrived at the airport and was presented with a white Mercedes by his company's officials—it was his predecessor's car. One of his new colleagues asked him a few days later how he liked the car, and Bob mentioned that he had never had a white car before or one with a stick shift. The next morning, he found the white Mercedes gone and in its place was a gray BMW with an automatic transmission.

It was a small thing, but it taught Bob a big lesson. The impact of whatever he said was amplified, especially in that initial break-in period when he was new and no one knew what to expect from him. Even the slightest hint that he might be unhappy with the car led to an immediate overreaction. What if he were to make a casual statement to his direct report that the person in charge of purchasing didn't get back to him yet—like the Mercedes, that person might be gone the next day.

Especially in your first month or two on the job, be highly conscious of any negative implications of your statements. Be alert to unintended consequences. As soon as you hear yourself thinking about reprimanding someone or expressing dissatisfaction in even the mildest form, consider how your people might overreact. If there are things taking place that truly are wrong and need correcting, then, of course, you need to call these to their attention. But save your criticism and other expressions of displeasure for these major issues.

Be conscious of not only what you say, but also of how you say it. Western leaders often react angrily or with disgust when things don't go their way. They may lose their temper with a direct report or allow their expressions and tone of voice to communicate their displeasure. In some cultures—the Middle East and Asia, especially—these negative tones and expressions are viewed as unbecoming for someone in a leadership role. People in those cultures expect leaders to be above these petty displays of pique. They want their leaders to project an aura of control, of being able to solve problems. When they see a leader berating a direct report or sneering at a memo that seems poorly prepared, they perceive the leader to be a petty tyrant.

This isn't to say that you can or should always remain cool and calm, but you should not come across as a bully, especially when the offenses are relatively minor. We should also note that in some developing countries the culture is more emotionally volatile than in others, and there leaders are expected to fly off the handle as well as provide extravagant praise. In some Latin American and Mediterranean countries, for instance, we've seen business owners and executives for whom shouting and hugging are normal modes of expression. Still, keep in mind that native leaders can get away with more than Western leaders can. As a general rule, what you say and how you say it will be magnified, and therefore keeping conscious control of how and what you communicate is advisable until your people get to know you better.

Now let's look at how you react to the way your employees, colleagues, and other individuals in a developing country communicate. Robert Knowling has an insightful take on this topic. Robert has been a telecommunications CEO who has worked extensively in Asia and Europe, has been on the board of Hewlett Packard, and is currently a consultant. He referred to the phenomenon that he terms "poker face" when he was working in Asia.

"Sometimes I've been in sessions where I haven't known if we were on the same page, and yet at the end of a meeting, I'd find out that they were completely in sync with me. Yet, throughout the session, I never understood where we were or even if we were on the same planet.... Their demeanor was much more subtle than anything I was used to.... There's a very big difference in terms of how we interact and conduct business in the United States versus how they do it in the Far East and elsewhere."

To expand on Robert's point: don't jump to conclusions based on how someone communicates or even based on what is said in a single interaction. While not all populations in developing countries adopt this poker-faced style, each country has its own signature ways of talking and reacting.

It takes a while to become familiar with a given country's style. For instance, in India and other countries, speakers often lavish praise on you—praise that may have an ulterior motive (someone wants to do a deal with you, obtain a raise, etc.). In Russia and some Eastern European countries, the style is more aggressive and even combative. Once you grasp what a particular style is, you'll realize that it's not necessarily a reaction to you or a situation but just a natural mode of communication in that culture.

Robert said that it took him a while to become accustomed to his Asian colleagues rarely gesturing or raising their voices in enthusiasm or anger. He referred to their style as subtle, in contrast to his own: "I have been coached to tone it down, to stay on an even keel, not to make a lot of gestures with my hands." It's disconcerting when you're speaking in a meeting using typical Western oratory and body language, and no one in your audience is reacting as you expected. Rather than jump to conclusions and figure that you've lost your audience, you need to recognize that you may be getting through to them even though the evidence isn't visible.

Show Respect through Communication

Most Western managers want to be respectful to their native employees, but they are inadvertently disrespectful. In many instances, they have failed to do their homework about essential communication courtesies and protocols in a given country. As a result, they commit social faux pas, ignore local customs, and use language that listeners find offensive or ignorant.

We understand that you can't completely avoid these unintentional mistakes, but you can follow certain guidelines that will increase the odds that you'll speak to your people in ways that don't offend:

Learn and Use at least a Few Key Phrases/Words

You don't have to become fluent in Arabic, Hindi, or any other language to be effective as a manager and leader in a developing country. Yet, if you make the effort to learn how to say hello or use a word that is in common usage in that country's business community or within the organization, you show your respect. For example, Bill, who was working in China, on his first day of work greeted his team by saying, "*ni hao.*" It made a huge impression on his staff that he had made the effort to learn the appropriate way to say hello in Mandarin Chinese. Bill said their faces lit up, and he found that getting off on the right foot made a huge difference in the transition period since his people were responsive to his requests and helpful with their suggestions. One of his colleagues who arrived from Australia at about the same time complained bitterly about how unfriendly and resistant his people were. Though there may have been more problems than this Australian's refusal to learn how to say even the simplest greeting in Mandarin, it struck Bill that small gestures can make a big difference in these situations.

In certain parts of Asia, people often start a conversation by asking, "Have you taken your dinner?" even first thing in the morning. It's their way of asking, "How are you?" Being aware of the ubiquity of this greeting and using it yourself can help you start conversations off the right way and convey that you respect your people's customs.

Every country and culture has a handful of signature phrases that relate to greetings, good-byes, expressions of gratitude, and compliments. Knowing the names of key national holidays, when they occur, and what to say to someone to acknowledge the holiday is another key learning. It doesn't take much time or practice to master these words, and it's a task that should be required of every executive who works in a developing country.

Recognize the Correct Way to Address People

Again, this is a simple way to show respect in communication. One of the essential pieces of knowledge is whether the country uses the surname first or second. For instance, when we worked in places like Korea, Japan, and China, people called us Johnson, Bob, and Oberwise, Rob. It may seem awkward to us, but to them it's the natural way of speaking, and we should respect it.

Similarly, the people you work with in a developing country may have titles that go beyond jobs and relate to their standing in a royal family, religion, or tribe. In Dubai, for instance, the highest member of the royal family is called His Royal Highness. Other members of the royal family are called Your Highness. Individuals who are members of the government are referred to as Your Excellence. Get these titles right and you earn respect; get them wrong or ignore them entirely, and you'll be viewed as an ignorant Westerner.

In some instances, you'll need to observe what natives of the country call each other to figure out the correct address. In Muslim countries, people sometimes use the full Muslim name; in some instances, they'll use shortened versions. Therefore, before making a slip, refrain from saying a name until you've heard it used by a native speaker. This will tip you off as to the correct address.

Finally, you'll probably be working with at least some highly educated colleagues who have acquired a PhD as part of their education. You'll find people are extraordinarily proud of this accomplishment, in no small part because they may have had to make far more sacrifices to obtain this degree than someone in the West would. They expect to be addressed as "Doctor," and you should honor their accomplishment by doing so.

Get the Pronunciation Right for Basic Words

Bob was brought to Dubai by Sheikh Mohammed bin Rashid Al Maktoum, one of the most powerful leaders in the Middle East, and his team of Dubai Inc. investors. On an initial occasion, he referenced what the sheikh had told him in meetings with his people, pronouncing it "sheek" as most Western people do. In fact, Bob learned to his great embarrassment that the correct pronunciation is "shake."

Don't make assumptions about key pronunciations. What is correct in the West may not be correct in a given country. Names of people, companies, and places (cities, countries, etc.) are especially important to get right, because when you say them wrong, it sounds almost as if you're making fun of a name even though that's not your intent.

Be Alert for the Subtle Signs that You're Communicating Disrespectfully

In most instances, these signs won't be obvious, making them easy to miss. Your people may accept your mispronunciations or your inability to say a single word in their language, but that doesn't make these behaviors acceptable. Be alert for the small, universal signs of displeasure: grimaces, frowns, sighs, slight shakes of the head. Watch, too, for blank looks—the spark of recognition and understanding is missing from their faces. If you see these responses repeatedly, try to figure out what particular thing you do or say that evokes them. If you are able to cultivate a trusted native advisor who will level with you, make sure he understands that you want to be informed if you're committing verbal errors that others find disrespectful.

Cultivate a QSR Approach

Question, simplify, repeat—that's the QSR approach, and it's one that is counterintuitive to many Western executives. Instead, we tend to favor the OCS-I-O approach: Order, complicate, say-it-once.

It's not that people in developing countries are any less intelligent than those in the West. It's that significant cultural and language barriers block effective communication. Even if your people speak your language, they may not grasp its nuances, and an inadvertent idiomatic expression can lead to confusion or misinterpretation. Similarly, they may not understand the specific protocol or concept you're trying to convey—you may ask them to test three concepts, but your idea of "test" and their cultural interpretation of "test" may be worlds apart.

In addition, consider the human capital maturity curve. We've referred to this concept before (and it's the subject of chapter 4), but it's an absolutely essential one in a variety of areas, including communication. If you're working with people who aren't particularly sophisticated when it comes to business practices and experiences, then what can be communicated quickly and almost automatically in the West requires greater explanation and patience in developing countries. In the West, we take maturity shortcuts—we say "supply chain management" and people know what we're talking about. You can't take such a shortcut in most developing countries.

For example, Amber, who was working in China for a large American fast-food restaurant chain, assigned her team a research project that entailed benchmarking best practices of competing fast-food establishments. Amber figured it was a relatively straightforward assignment, and she was pleased when her team seemed to respond enthusiastically to the task. She asked them to have the report completed in three weeks, but the deadline passed without a report. She convened the team and asked why she hadn't received the report. The team hemmed and hawed and finally admitted that not only did they not have the report but they had not done any of the benchmarking required to create the report. At first Amber was furious, but as her people talked to her, she realized that they had not understood the assignment. They had assumed that if Amber considered it a high priority, she would have been monitoring them constantly since that is how their native bosses operated. For years, they had prioritized based on how insistent their boss was about a given project. To them, Amber's silence after the initial meeting indicated that she was not particularly concerned about the report.

When we interviewed one of the leaders working in a developing country, he suggested that neophyte managers in these countries should assume that "they are speaking through a bunch of invisible screens that filter out at least some of what they want to communicate." These managers may think they've conveyed the urgency of project, the specifics about how they want it accomplished, and the final outcome they hope for , but the language and cultural barriers we alluded to earlier filter out at least some of these messages.

Therefore, the first thing you need to do is ask questions. In developed countries, most direct reports will ask clarifying questions if you haven't communicated something clearly. This is less likely to happen in the developing areas of the world. Even if you tell people in these countries that they should ask if they don't understand something, they may fail to do so, thinking that you really don't want questions and are just being polite.

The goal of your questions should be to assess their understanding of what you've requested. More specifically, ask whether they grasp

- what action you want them to take,
- what the deadline is,
- who should do what, and
- what tangible outcome you are looking for (a report, a white paper, a list of recommendations, etc.).

Next, concentrate on simplifying your explanations and assignments. A number of people we interviewed noted that when they first started working in a developing country, they felt they needed to provide extremely detailed instructions and explanations to overcome language and cultural barriers. In fact, they discovered they were overwhelming their people with information. One of the biggest mistakes is asking them to do something and then provide them with responses for each and every contingency: If the customer refuses to add a new line, try x; if the customer is somewhat open to the new line, try y; if the customer is somewhat resistant, try z. People often become sidetracked by contingency planning and lose the main point you're trying to communicate.

At the beginning of your tenure, then, simplify your requests and explanations. We know this can be challenging because you want to help your people benefit from your experience and expertise, but it's better to err on the side of simplicity rather than complexity. As time goes on and you learn the best ways to communicate with your staff, you can add another level of detail. For now, though, keep in mind the adage that less is more.

When we suggest repeating things, we're advocating the old Madison Avenue advertising method: Say it once, and then say it again. To avoid beating your people over the head with the point you want to make, don't become "obviously" repetitive. For example: "I don't want you to contact George on this project; I repeat, don't contact George!" Instead, find a fresh way to say the same thing: "I don't want you to contact George on this project. I realize that you've worked closely with George in the past, but for this project, at least, he might prove to be an obstacle if he's involved."

Repetition can be handled in ways that don't make the other party feel stupid or bored. You want to repeat your points to be sure you communicate your intent, but a bit of creative wordsmithery will help the repetition go down easier.

Little Things Count

We've noticed that business leaders from the United States, Europe, and other modernized countries like to communicate big things. They want to talk about their philosophy, their long-range strategy, and their values. There's nothing wrong with any of this, except in many developing countries, these executives are talking about issues that are only of peripheral interest to the people who live and work there. This goes back to Maslow's hierarchy of needs: If you're focusing on survival, you're not going to care much about self-actualization.

Again, we're not suggesting that your people will all be one step away from the breadline—you no doubt will have direct reports who are as smart and as educated as anyone in your own country—but you may be dealing with people who are much more concerned about the survival of the company than the CEO's vision for the future. It may not have been that long ago that their countries were embroiled in wars or beset by economic chaos, so they are much more pragmatic and focused in their perspectives than employees in developed nations where the business environment has been relatively stable for years.

One of the most common communication mistakes new leaders in developing countries make is giving speeches about return on investment, strategic imperatives, and building sustainable enterprises. During the talk, they look at their audience and see a bunch of people whose eyes have glazed over. Or afterward they talk to members of the audience and realize their speech didn't have the impact they had hoped for. The problem is that in many developing countries, the purpose of business is nothing as grand as building a sustainable enterprise. For people there, business is about job creation, about employing people at decent wages for a reasonable length of time. So what people respond to is talk of 2,000 new jobs created annually or 10 percent annual increases in salary based on a given rate of growth.

For example, a midsized company based in the United Kingdom had a plant in South America, and there was a growing chasm between management and the line employees. Most of the managers were from the United Kingdom or other Western countries while most of the line employees were from South America. The new CEO alternated between motivational talks ("We're all in this together") and threats ("I'll fire all of you!"). Communication deteriorated, as did the level of trust. Production at the plant suffered, and within a year the company replaced the CEO with Andrew, a veteran of companies operating in South America as well as other developing countries.

Andrew sat down with a number of representatives from the plant and asked what the line employees really wanted. Surprisingly, pay increases and improved benefits weren't their major priorities. Instead, they talked about wanting better food in the plant's cafeteria, wanting better lighting in the factory parking lot for the night shift workers, and wanting to control the music that played over the loudspeakers in the factory. There were a lot of little things causing problems rather than one or two big things.

Andrew responded immediately by granting all their small requests. Almost immediately, the communication and trust levels improved. Just as important, so did productivity.

Unlike the previous CEO, Andrew recognized that as much as the employees might want increased salaries, bonuses, and so on, they were realistic about what was possible—more realistic, in some ways, than their Western counterparts. What mattered most to them were little things regarding which they felt they could and should have some input.

For this reason, if you want to communicate well with your people, ask them what things bug them about their working environment. The odds are that they will have a long list of grievances, many of which can be addressed quickly and inexpensively. It may be that they want free tea and not just free coffee, or perhaps they want a better brand of coffee. It may be that they want the company to sponsor their soccer team. It may be that they want the temperature in the factory or office lowered a bit during the hot, humid season.

Don't dismiss these small requests as trivial. They are anything but trivial for the people who are making them. These small things represent your opportunity to establish lines of communication that might otherwise be closed to you.

Assess Your Communication Skills

Being conscious of communicating in the ways we've discussed can make a huge difference in your success in a developing country. In many ways, communication behaviors are the easiest for Western managers to adjust. These adjustments don't require a great deal of new learning or major shifts in attitudes. What they do require is being aware of the traps that Western executives fall into and the actions that earn them trust and respect in foreign lands.

To foster this awareness, here are some key questions to keep asking yourself when you find yourself trying to communicate effectively in a developing nation:

- Are you patient with your direct reports even when you're unclear about what they're trying to say? Do you encourage them to explain and ask them questions designed to help them? Or do you cut them short and decide that what they have to say isn't that important?
- Do you tend to do a lot more talking than listening? Do you find yourself in the role of an authority figure everyone looks to for answers? Or are you able to step away from this role and communicate that you don't have all the answers and you need their help?
- Do you find it difficult to listen to your people because you're completely overwhelmed with all the problems and confusions of operating in a country very different from what you're used to? Or do you take advantage of the times when things calm down a bit and make an effort to hear what you're people are trying to tell you?
- Do you often say things without thinking and find that employees overreact to your criticism or give you far more than you asked for? Or do you attempt to keep your words and gestures under control, to maintain a calm and even disposition?
- Have you made the effort to learn at least a few key words/phrases in your new country's language? Do you know the correct way to address certain colleagues and customers who are members of the royal family, religious leaders, or have other titles? Have you investigated how to pronounce certain words (names of people you work with, for instance)?

- Are you more likely to give orders than make requests politely?
- Do you tend to give long-winded perorations rather than make concise statements?
- Do you expect people to understand what you're saying immediately after the first time you say it?
- Do you sweat the small stuff when it comes to communication? Do you make an effort to find out and discuss the daily frustrations and wants of your people?

CHAPTER 3

Become a Leader of Both Tribes and Individuals

L eaders in developing countries often are confused about what their people expect from them and what they can expect from their people. Western managers come into these foreign environments with the following assumptions:

- People may have personality conflicts with other employees, but they will generally treat their colleagues with a fair and open-minded approach.
- Employees will draw a clear line between their professional and personal lives.
- The primary role of leaders/managers is to grow the company and their people; employees don't need to know them or like them, but they need to respect them.

- Employees will follow corporate rules and adhere to company values.
- Loyalty to the organization supersedes loyalty to any other group during the work day.

All these assumptions may be wrong, and the first five sections of this chapter will address each of them. Tribal cultures (and we're using the word "tribal" in the broadest possible sense to describe all powerful networks external to a company), especially, are not compatible with the traditional social dynamic of an organization. In countries with a history of tribes, religious sects, royalty, and other groups that wield a powerful influence over people's lives, individual employees don't think or act the way employees in a Western country do. They may relate to a boss much like they relate to religious leaders or powerful members of the royal family. They may expect a company to accommodate them in terms of their religious beliefs and practices. Therefore, understanding the realities behind these often false assumptions can greatly improve leadership and management effectiveness. To that end, let's look at the first assumption and the truth many Western managers in developing countries eventually learn.

Tribal Disputes Can Cause Dissension and Even Sabotage

When Bob was running Dubai Aerospace Enterprises, it took him a while to realize that certain members of his team sometimes seemed more concerned with besting each other than with carrying out their tasks effectively. What he didn't realize was that certain members of his diverse team hated each other because their countries of origin had a long history of being enemies, and some team members had different religious affiliations that caused them to disdain each other.

Even more subtly, though, he had two people who reported to him who were part of the same royal family, but they were intensely competitive with each other—so much so that they would expend time and energy plotting against each other. Unfortunately, there were projects where they had to work on together, and Bob sometimes had to spend more time refereeing their disputes than managing the team. At one point, one of these individuals was put in jail, and the rival employee called Bob to gloat over his enemy's fate.

Obviously, there's not much you can do about tribal competitiveness or disputes, some of which have origins in the distant past. What you can do, however, is find someone you trust who is native to the country in which you're working and ask the following questions:

- What particular religious, tribal, or other sectarian groups don't get along?
- How intense is the feud between these two groups; is it sufficiently intense that two individuals from these groups cannot work together?
- Do you know of any individuals you feel should not work together because of their tribal or other affiliations?

At the same time, don't automatically assume that members of feuding groups can't work together. In many cases, we've found that savvy leaders can mediate disputes and convince people to subordinate their animosity to the greater good of a team or an organization. For instance, John was heading a team for a multinational company in Mumbai a few years ago, and he became aware that one member of the team seemed to be snubbing another during meetings. It turned out that the snubber was a member of the Brahman caste and the "snubbee" was a member of the Dalit or untouchables. When John understood the source of the problem—he talked to an Indian member of the government who explained the historical basis of the caste system and how the prejudices inherent in it were different from the racism that John initially compared it to—he sat down with the Brahman and explained that this behavior couldn't continue. It turned out that the Brahman was not even aware that he was snubbing his fellow team member—at least according to him, his attitude was unconscious. From that point on, he made an effort to be cordial and communicative toward the Dalit member of his team.

Blurred Boundaries Must Be Negotiated

In most organizations in Western countries, people observe boundaries that divide the personal and the professional. In many instances, it takes years before a direct report introduces his boss to his family. When the workday is done, company leaders and their employees go their separate ways. Perhaps even more significantly, people tend to keep their private lives private. In other words, bosses know relatively little about what employees do in their off-hours and vice versa. It's not a total separation—executives may get together for a round of golf, and a boss may know some basic information about a direct report and her family—but boundaries exist and are usually observed.

In many developing countries, these boundaries are nonexistent. This doesn't mean that the assembly line worker in the factory is best friends with the CEO but that employees expect there to be a certain amount of communication and interaction that is personal and not just professional. People join organizations for more than a job or the salary or the work itself. What they want are relationships. In countries like the United States, individualism is the norm. As a result, people in organizations tend not to want as much social interaction or strong personal relationships—they satisfy these requirements outside the organization. In countries with strong tribal cultures, however, social relationships are of paramount importance in all areas of life, including work.

Francis Yuen, the CEO we met in chapter 2, found to his surprise when he first started working in China that he could not really work effectively with people there until he had established friendships with his direct reports and colleagues. While in the West people generally work with others on a purely professional level, this was not the case in China. As Francis explained, "It takes a couple of sessions together before they start to consider you as somebody they want to talk to and can be friendly to. In those days, and to a certain extent now, friendship comes first, before business. That is primarily because they want to asses you, and they want to see if you're someone they can trust."

When Rob was working in China, he found that the people he was working with often asked him to join them for dinner and made it a point to introduce him to members of their particular tribes—family, friends, and government officials. They wanted to get to know him, but they also wanted him to get to know the people they knew. This was their social etiquette, and they judged him not just in terms of his skill as a business person but by who he was as a person.

Bob, too, experienced a similar situation in Dubai. One of his team members was Fayyad, one of his investors and a man who was close to the royal family. In the middle of a work day, he stopped by Bob's office and said that he wanted to show him the historic parts of Dubai and how people used to live before the city was modernized. It was a brutally hot day, but Bob realized that Fayyad attached great importance to this field trip, and so he agreed to it. They went out in their suits and walked through the stifling heat to an old section of the city, and Fayyad gave Bob a tour of homes that seemed unchanged from how they must have appeared over a hundred years ago. He then took Bob to his own house and introduced him to his family. He wanted Bob to gain an appreciation for who he was as a person and who Dubai's citizens were as people. He didn't see anything wrong with leaving the office during a busy workday to achieve this goal. For him, it was integral to establishing a productive working relationship.

In talking to other managers who have worked in developing countries around the world, we collected a number of stories related to how people broke down the barriers between professional and personal. Here are some examples:

- An employee confessed that he loves a fellow employee who refused his proposal of marriage; he asked his boss to intercede on his behalf.

- Outings to cultural events were planned, such as plays, music, and movies.
- Family gatherings were held to which the boss is expected to bring his family members to meet a direct report's or colleague's family members.
- Requests were made to attend a religious ceremony.
- Complex and sometimes confusing family quarrels were discussed and advice requested.

We're not telling you to accede to all requests or that you have to provide your people with detailed information and access to your personal life. Your willingness to blur the lines between personal and professional to some extent, however, can go a long way toward gaining your employees' acceptance. Therefore, make an effort to be more open about your life when you talk to direct reports. At least a few times a year, make a point of scheduling outside social interactions with your people and perhaps their families. Be willing to talk with your people about personal issues that you might not talk about in a Western company. Accept that you might feel a little uncomfortable at first in these situations but that you'll gain respect and a better understanding of the people you work with.

Understand, too, the value of learning to form stronger relationships with your people. As many leaders in the United States and other Western nations have learned, they can no longer rely only on the power of their position to get people to work to the best of their abilities. Employees, especially younger ones, resent being ordered to carry out a task or being treated as a faceless functionary. They want to be acknowledged as individuals, and only then will they be fully committed to the tasks they're assigned.

In developing countries, leaders have the opportunity to fine-tune their relationship-building skills. They need to communicate better with direct reports, to socialize with them, to get to know who they are as individuals and not just as employees. There is no magic to building this skill, but it does require practice, and most leadership positions in developing countries provide situations for a lot of practice in this area. The next section will describe what types of activities to practice.

It Is a Popularity Contest

The opposite of what this subheading refers to is a favorite saying of Western managers when they're told that their people don't like them. They respond, "It's not a popularity contest; I want them to respect me, and I don't care if they don't like me." We're not sure how valid this approach is even in the West—it was more appropriate for the command-and-control era—but it often fails in developing countries.

Again, it's not that people there want or expect to be best friends with the boss. In countries with histories of royal or tribal leaders, people are accustomed to being extremely deferential to kings and other heads of various entities. But they also expect to see, meet, and know about these esteemed individuals. They want to be informed about the king's preferences in clothing styles, and they expect the local tribal leader to show up at their village festival. When people in developing nations join a company, it becomes another tribe. They want to feel they belong, and the organizational managers and leaders who foster this sense of belonging will fare far better than those who do not. We've heard stories about leaders who came into companies in developing nations and adjusted well to cultural differences and learned how to do business effectively in foreign environments, but they never captured the hearts and minds of their employees. They revealed little of themselves, rarely mingled with anyone except the senior members of their team and didn't encourage other Western managers to interact with their direct reports. The result was a lack of energy and commitment, leading to decreased productivity.

In our interviews, a number of executives told stories indicating that drinking with employees has benefits. Milt, for instance, was doing a consulting project for a company in Russia, and he and his Russian client worked for a solid week in the Ukraine with very few breaks. Then, when the project was finished, the client took him to the home of a village elder where a number of community members were seated around a table with a bottle of vodka standing in the center. Milt and his client also sat down, and they began a conversation in which you could not talk until you first took a drink of vodka—every utterance was preceded by a drink. Milt found it to be an almost ritualistic process, but he discovered that his participation cemented his relationship with his client in ways that none of their work during the week had done.

Mark told us the story of going to work for a South Korean automobile company, and during his first week there, his boss and a few other executives invited him out for drinks. The ritual here was that you pour your neighbor's drink from a bottle on the table when his glass is empty. Later, Mark learned that the purpose of this ritual wasn't to get drunk but to help loosen people up so they could start building open and honest relationships.

Drinking, though, is not the only or the best way to let people get to know you (and in some developing countries, alcohol consumption is frowned upon or even forbidden). When Bob worked in Singapore, he took over an organization that had poor morale and productivity. During his first month there, Bob examined a variety of alternatives to improve both, but before he decided on a particular course of action, the solution presented itself to him. One of his direct reports entered his office and told him it was time to plan the company's dinner dance. Bob asked what that was and was informed that this was an annual, formal event that all 1,500 company employees attended. The direct report told him that the previous leadership team had also attended this event but had not participated in any of the activities. Bob wondered what activities he was referring to. He was informed that traditionally, everyone participates in the games and skits that are part of the dinner dance—from egg tosses to musical numbers (clearly, this was a different type of dinner dance than is held in the West). Bob's direct report also explained that the previous Western management team merely observed rather than participated in these activities. Bob could tell that this direct report had been disappointed in their lack of participation and that others had also been disappointed.

So Bob decided that not only would his management team participate in the various games but they would also do a skit—the first year he and his team donned white gloves on one hand and sang and danced a Michael Jackson tune; the next year they put on cowboy hats and sang cowboy songs.

Bob and his team also made an effort to join in extracurricular activities that CEOs rarely do—he joined the company bowling team, for instance.

The result was a gradual but significant improvement in communication throughout the company. Morale, too, rose. People were more willing to volunteer their suggestions and to participate on new teams. They also took more risks with the projects they proposed—they were less fearful of making mistakes. As you might expect, productivity and profitability increased as well.

We're not suggesting that the participation of CEOs and other leaders in various "fun" activities has an instant or magical effect. What it does do, though, is get the ball rolling. In other words, a given group of employees in a developing country will have uncertainty, if not outright hostility, regarding their new Western managers. It's natural that they should feel a bit like being in occupied territory and resent the conquerors, no matter who owns the company or how friendly relationships are with the West. There's still the sense that the Western people are outsiders. For the insiders to make a commitment to the company, they need to feel like it's worth it. They start to feel this way when they like who their new leader is, when they feel he or she is making an effort to let his or her hair down and to be a sport. This humanizes their leader, and it helps others relate to him or her.

We would urge you to make a similar effort by doing the following:

- Ask questions about a former Western leader who occupied your position (or was in another managerial slot); find out if he was liked or disliked. If the latter, find

out what about him irritated people; determine if native employees found him cold and distant or at least unwilling to let others get to know him.
- Based on what you learn, make an effort not to follow in a disliked Western leader's footsteps; think about what you can do to be more transparent as a person and as a leader.
- Find out what a favorite activity is for employees—sports, dining out, playing cards—and join in at least a few times annually.
- Consider joining your colleagues for drinks if this is part of their cultural way of communicating.

Allegiance to Cultural Norms
Can Impact Corporate Rules

It's not that people in developing countries ignore corporate rules. It's simply that cultural norms are so powerful that they may influence how these rules are interpreted. Western managers in these countries sometimes forget that organizational policies and procedures are formed based on a Western mind-set. Everything from the nine-to-five workday to coffee breaks to hiring protocols is based on certain aspects of the societies in which the companies evolved. The expectation is that people will follow the rules; no manager would look kindly on someone who decided to work his own idiosyncratic hours.

When Bob was working in Singapore, one of his managers came into his office and informed him that they needed to fire an employee. Bob asked why. The manager explained that this employee was discovered napping on his shift. Bob started asking "Western mentality" questions: Was the employee sick? The manager said it didn't matter. Then Bob asked whether the guy had family problems, and again the manager responded that it didn't matter. Perhaps they had been pushing the employee too hard, and he was overworked and tired. Again, the manager said that it didn't matter.

Finally, Bob said, "I get it. It doesn't matter. But why doesn't it matter?"

The manager explained that their work ethic dictated that sleeping at work was forbidden, and if they didn't enforce it, then everyone would sleep at work. If this employee couldn't stay awake, he shouldn't have come to work.

In other words, a cultural norm had become an unofficial company rule.

In many instances in developing countries, cultural norms and values filter into the workplace. A number of executives who worked in Middle Eastern countries noted that they learned the importance of providing regular breaks for prayers; their people were going to take these breaks no matter what, and it made sense to accommodate their religious requirements. People were willing to make up the time at other points in the day in order to receive prayer time.

You may perceive these prayer time breaks as impediments to productivity. In fact, they are essential to achieve good levels of productivity since if you forbid these breaks, employees will never work as hard as they are capable of working. Think of how it would be if you were a manager of a company in the Bible Belt, and you insisted that all employees must work Sunday mornings. We've talked to managers in developing countries who have noted the importance of providing breaks for meditation and for siestas and days off when national or local soccer teams are playing. None of this may seem important to us, but these breaks are as essential to native employees as coffee breaks are to workers in the United States.

Hiring is another area where a country's norms can have a major influence on organizational rules. While the human resources manager or whoever is responsible for hiring will probably consider which candidate best fits the job specs, he or she may also give priority to candidates who "know someone." In some instances, family members such as siblings and cousins are pushed to the top of the list, regardless of their qualifications. In other instances, qualified candidates are hired over other qualified candidates because they knew someone of influence within the organization. Though this type of hiring decision also happens in the West, it is much more common—and sometimes much more overt—in developing countries. In fact, it's not unusual to find organizations in these countries where five, ten, or more employees are all related to each other. Again, don't expect to eliminate nepotism. Instead, your goal should be to make sure that if friends or family members are hired, they're reasonably well qualified—or if they're not, you should have a good training program to get them up to speed as quickly as possible.

To deal with the influence of these cultural norms effectively, here are some suggestions:

- Focus on the rules or policies in your organization that strike you as anomalous from a Western perspective.

- Analyze whether the rule or policy has a negative impact on the company's productivity or profitability.
- Consulting with a trusted native employee, determine how ingrained the rule or policy is from a cultural perspective and the harm it would do if it were changed.
- If you determine any change would result in more harm than good, leave it alone; if you can modify the rule or policy without serious resentment and minimize the negative impact, consider this your best alternative.

Outside Connections May Influence Inside Decisions

As a manager, you may tell your people to go with the lowest bidder, or you may provide guidelines on how to choose a supplier, or you may explain the protocols necessary for obtaining government approval for a project. But none of this may have much of an effect on how people actually make choices. Instead, they are influenced by their connections.

They will award a contract to a vendor who is a member of their tribe, sect, or family.

They will do an end run around standard procedures when seeking government approval and get a project green-lighted based on a phone call to their brother-in-law who is a government functionary. They will recommend an area for construction not because it is the optimum piece of real estate, but because it will enable a tribal member to sell land he owns.

The problem is that if you're coming into a company and a developing country as a greenhorn, none of this may be apparent to you at first. For example, Tom, who worked for an energy company in Russia as a purchasing manager, said that at first his people's purchasing decisions seemed incomprehensible. He couldn't figure out why one member of his team would require a government official to accompany him on every trip to negotiate a purchase of equipment or why another member of his team insisted that a particular supplier provided much higher quality equipment than any other, and yet this was an area where that company had the highest rate of defects.

For months, no one would level with him about these and other matters. It was only when he was back in the United States and meeting with a former Russian employee of the energy company that he learned that his people were loyal first and foremost to a tight-knit network of government officials and private citizens who controlled sales of heavy equipment in the region. This network determined who bought what from whom, and his people received a kickback from suppliers. The former employee told this purchasing manager that there was no way to go around this network without serious repercussions, and that the best policy was to meet with a representative of this network to ensure that they provided the company with quality suppliers—this would entail a certain amount of wining and dining, but it was a realistic goal. Tom took this ex-employee's advice and found that after a few weeks of expensive dinners, the purchases his group made resulted in a significant quality improvement.

The lesson here is to make an effort as soon as possible to determine where your employees' loyalties lie outside the company. You can't assume that people will make decisions independent of any outside group. In fact, you probably should assume that the odds are at least even that they will be influenced by outsiders. Again, we're not making a judgment, and neither should you. But it pays to be aware of who your key people are connected with and how.

In Dubai, though Bob met frequently with the sheikh and had a good relationship with him, he required additional eyes and ears who could keep him abreast of how government and tribal influencers were affecting the decisions his people made. Bob did this by forming a relationship with one member of his team who was well-connected with the royal family and hiring two other people who could provide him with the lay of the land.

Hiring people with governmental connections, therefore, is a good tactic to monitor how that particular group might be impacting employee choices. Forming your own relationship with a government, tribal, or religious leader is also a good tactic, though this can take time, and your access to the most powerful members of a given group can be limited by circumstances as well as by your own position within an organization (if you're not a CEO or country manager, access may be difficult).

It's also possible that your people will level with you about their outside influences, but this can take time and trust. In fact, a number of executives in developing countries have told us that people lied to them about their relationship with a government official or sect leader. They denied that these individuals influenced who they gave business to or who they hired, even when it was obvious that a connection existed. So even though it's fine to have this type of conversation with your people, it may not yield much information in some instances.

Multilevel Management

"Things aren't always what they seem."

"You need two sets of eyes—one to see what's going on in front of you, one to see what's going on behind the scenes."

"Sometimes I felt like all my conversations with direct reports and customers and suppliers were just for show; that the real game was being played when I wasn't around."

These quotes from Western managers who worked in developing countries are indicative of what we refer to as the "multilevel game." There's the content level where what you see is what you get—it's the day-to-day meetings, assignments of tasks, reports, and so on. But there's also a hidden process where everything that happened during the day is filtered; a combination of outside influencers as well as cultural imperatives can reshape what took place at the content level.

The multilevel game poses problems for Western managers accustomed to working at one level. Yet to be successful, managers need to think in multilevel terms. As noted in the previous section, people can be working for two managers: you and the person outside the organization in whose network they operate. But these levels are more complex than just that. There's also the issue of a tribal consciousness, which dictates that the relationship with a manager is far more complex than the traditional dynamic between manager and direct report.

We've found that direct reports in developing countries often were far more sensitive than their Western counterparts to both praise and criticism. If you seem to favor one person over another with an assignment or simply a positive remark, that person is elated, and his colleagues are devastated (to be left out). If you spend ten minutes with one person going over his project and twenty minutes with another employee, the former will feel slighted and the latter will feel favored. So you shouldn't be surprised if the next day the individual who feels slighted comes to work with a chip on his shoulder or seems unduly reticent or depressed.

In many of these countries, people measure themselves based on their relationship to the person in power—the local priest, sect leader, king, tribal head, and so on. They often measure their value in an organization based on their relationship to their boss. As a result, they are constantly interpreting and reassessing where they stand in relation to their managers. Their behaviors at work—their sudden enthusiasms, their lack of commitment—all are related to this interpreting and reassessing.

Is a multiple level game going on in your organization? While not every company in every developing country has this issue—and while it can be more intense in some situations than others—we've found it be a relatively common occurrence. Therefore, you need to assess whether it exists; the more affirmative responses you give to the following questions, the more likely it's an issue you'll have to address:

- Do you know or believe that your direct reports are providing an outside person—a government official, a community leader, a member of religious group—with information about what's taking place in your organization?
- Have you ever witnessed direct influence on corporate policies and programs by someone outside the organization?

- In your developing country, does a dictatorship exist? Or is there a highly powerful central government, religious group, or other entity that seems to control everything that happens within the country's borders?
- Do your people react differently than employees in the West to both criticism and praise? Do they seem over-sensitive at times and insensitive on other occasions?
- Have you ever assigned a direct report a task and it seemed he was highly resentful, either because of the way you assigned it or because of the nature of the task itself?
- Have you ever assigned a direct report a task or had a conversation with him and been confused by his reaction, whether positive or negative? Did he seem to be reacting to something in his head rather than something you said or did?

If you answered yes to some or all of these questions, investigate the context; determine if your people have private reservations about your requests or feedback. We've found that managers who are native to these countries are natural multilevel thinkers; they intuitively know that they have to be aware of all these aspects in order to motivate people and get them to stay on task. Western leaders need to develop the same mentality, and here are three ways for them to do so:

- Make a conscious effort to manage in multiple dimensions. Easier said than done, we know, but just raising your awareness that more is going on than meets the eye can help a lot. Don't take things at face value. When you see your employees reacting in ways that don't make sense, try to investigate what's going on—talk to them as well as others who might be honest with you. Ask direct reports about their relationships with religious groups, family-based entities, tribal society, and the like. Again, not everyone will be completely up-front, but perhaps a few of them will provide you with insights.

- Learn about the key networks within the country. Talk to locals about where the real power in the country lies—government, family, tribe. The more you learn— who the network leaders are, what their interests are, how those interests intersect with your business—the more you'll be able to deal with them effectively. You may discover that 90 percent of the employees hired in the past year are from one of these networks. You may be surprised to find that a particular government official receives regular reports of what goes on in your company meetings. This knowledge is important since it can help you avoid trying to accomplish tasks that are never going to be accomplished (because they're not in the best interest of a particular outside group).

- Find a local "interpreter." We're not referring to someone who can translate the local language but to an individual who can help you interpret people's reactions to what you say and do as a manager, someone who is keenly aware of how outside networks impact your people and the moves your company wants to make. While it's great if this individual is employed by your company, you may need to venture outside of it to find your interpreter.

We recognize that multilevel managing is one of the more challenging tasks for Western managers in developing countries. It may seem like this is more trouble than it's worth, that the culture you're dealing with is too complex to grasp. In fact, it's just different. Both of us, like many other people we interviewed, found that with a bit of initiative and persistence, multilevel management can be learned and applied effectively.

CHAPTER 4

Assess the Human Capital Maturity Curve

Human capital maturity is a concept we mentioned briefly in chapter 2, but it's an absolutely critical—and often overlooked—concept for managers who want to be successful in developing countries. In the West, we typically assume that our employees possess a certain degree of experience, that they've acquired a basic level of savvy and skills. We believe that most if not all of them understand the rules of getting work done in an organization—that they know how to behave in various organizational settings, how to turn out work in a timely fashion, what to do if they don't understand something, and so on. A curve can be plotted for every organization to represent the combined maturity of all employees. If your human capital is at the top of the curve, your organization is full of people who are savvy about business concepts, emotionally intelligent, and willing and able to learn. If your human capital is at the bottom of the curve, many of the employees in your organization have not yet mastered essential business knowledge and skills, often act arrogantly or rudely, and are not adept learners. In most Western companies, the human capital is often at least in the middle of the curve (if not higher) because most employees have acquired sufficient knowledge through education, experience, and acculturation to function with some degree of maturity.

In developing countries, however, employees are generally lower on the human capital maturity curve than in the West—sometimes much lower. In certain instances, their lack of maturity is obvious—they ignore deadlines or seem incapable of adhering to stated work hours. In other instances, however, their lack of maturity is not obvious initially. They often possess excellent educational credentials, whether from their own country or the West, and it appears that at least some of the people who are direct reports or in managerial roles are highly competent. In fact, many of these individuals may lack the experience necessary to develop the maturity of their Western counterparts. They may be very intelligent and even highly skilled, but they operate in ways that betray immaturity—they are slow to learn new skills or have problems tailoring their approach to changing conditions, for example. You need to be aware of the level of maturity of your people. More than that, you must assess this level and then take steps to increase it if it's too low. This is true whether you're just managing a few people or are responsible for an entire workforce.

Before getting to how to conduct this assessment, we need to define our terms. Specifically, what is human capital maturity in specific, measurable terms?

Three Kinds of Maturity

Most managers evaluate the quality of their people primarily based on experience and expertise, which is fine in the West. Obviously, these two factors are important in developing countries as well. But in India, China, Russia, and other similar parts of the world, human capital maturity is more complex. For this reason, we've identified three areas that will help you assess human capital maturity in developing countries:

Business Savvy Maturity

It's astonishing how many people in developing countries have never worked on a team or have little experience operating with deadlines or don't have a good grasp of supply chain dynamics. Even more surprising, a significant percentage of these employees have never worked within a system. In other words, they are mystified by processes, and they struggle to understand how their specific tasks fit into a larger framework. While people in the West usually see how their individual efforts contribute to a larger whole, this connection isn't always apparent to people in developing countries. They are accustomed to seeing the direct result of their work—a report produced, a plan implemented—but often are unaware of the ramifications of that work for other divisions or for the company as a whole.

Consequently, they may become disconnected from their work and dispirited about what they're doing. For example, Miguel worked in a Latin American country for a midsized company based in Europe, and he had grown up in a village in the Amazonian jungle. Miguel, though, was exceptionally intelligent and had acquired an engineering degree by the time he was thirty. He was hired by the company as part of its effort to have a greater percentage of employees from the local population. Miguel was highly competent at his quality control position, traveling throughout South American countries and troubleshooting problems at the company's various factories. But after working for the company for little more than a year, he abruptly resigned. It turned out that Miguel felt like he was working in a vacuum. Factory managers rarely followed up with him about his work at their plant; he didn't understand the value of his recommendations and whether his reports were heeded or even read. Though he liked his boss (from the company's European headquarters) and his boss found him to be a conscientious, skilled employee, Miguel was often bewildered by the assignments he received. He didn't understand why he was asked to address a quality issue at one plant and a different quality issue at another and how or why these assignments were made. From a cultural standpoint, Miguel was reluctant to ask questions—he grew up in a village culture where unquestioning obedience to authority was the rule. And so, after a period of time, he resigned because he was getting little sense of accomplishment or affiliation from his work. The system in which he was functioning was strange to him, and no one ever bothered to address this issue.

Emotional Maturity

We're using this term in a broad sense. In any company in any country, there will be individuals who are more adult in their behavior than others—they take more responsibility, they deal better with conflict, and so on. In developing countries, however, a sizable number of employees are further down on the emotional maturity curve in that they don't know how to behave within an organizational culture. Some people, like Miguel, don't know when it's appropriate to ask questions. Some are naive and don't know when a boss is joking or being serious. And still others are immature by being overly egotistical in their interactions. We should also emphasize that emotional immaturity can occur at all levels and even at the top, as the following story illustrates.

In Dubai, Habib came up with the idea for Dubai Aerospace Enterprise, the company that recruited Bob to be its CEO. It was a bold, visionary concept for an organization, and Habib's status as a veteran of this industry and his articulation of the concept helped launch Dubai Aerospace. This company was integral to the sheikh's plan to turn Dubai into the epicenter of business in this part of the world, and it would provide an industrial and educational base to do so. As part of the royal family, having been well-educated in the West, and as an aerospace specialist, Habib had a lot going for him and should have been a huge asset to Dubai Aerospace once it was launched.

Yet his ego got in the way. He thought that because it was his idea, he was entitled to be CEO despite his lack of business experience (and his lack of broad-based experience—he was still under thirty). Still, he was given a prominent position within Dubai Aerospace and was being groomed for a leadership role. The idea was to rotate him through various jobs so he could acquire the business knowledge he was missing. Unfortunately, Habib's ego prevented him from agreeing to this plan. Even worse, it turned him into a scheming presence—for example, he was constantly trying to get his name in the newspapers and thus created animosity among his fellow executives. Eventually, his behaviors prompted other employees to try to sabotage him, and the internecine competition became a drain on the company's resources.

In many developing countries, native people who are appointed to top positions often have been educated in the West and grew up in highly privileged environments. What some of them lack, however, is the seasoning that comes from starting at the bottom and working one's way up. They have had their road paved for them, and their experiences have not matured them.

Learning Maturity

More subtle than the two criteria mentioned above, learning maturity is both the willingness to acquire new skills and knowledge and the ability to change habits and patterns in order to learn. In the West, we're taught to be constant learners. Even after we graduate from school, we're encouraged to learn more via seminars and workshops or through other methods. Training, executive development, and coaching are key components of most large Western companies, and the premise behind these functions is that people need to continue to educate themselves no matter what their career stage might be. Of course, not all employees in the West respond positively to this learning imperative—some prefer to coast and some don't like to take the risks associated with learning. Nonetheless, our culture espouses business learning, and a significant percentage of people respond positively to this cultural norm.

In some developing countries, though, this attitude toward learning hasn't been inculcated. This is especially true for people born into wealth and royalty. In some instances, a sense of entitlement develops, and people don't see the need to be aggressive, lifelong learners. There are many exceptions to this rule, especially among people not born into privileged status. And some cultures prize learning more than others. Among the royals in Dubai, Bob found a number of people who were mature learners, such as Abdul, who demonstrated an eagerness for learning new business skills and had the humility to accept coaching gratefully.

Humility, though, is the key word when it comes to this type of maturity. To learn means admitting that you don't know something, and in some cultures such an admission represents a loss of face. We've seen executives in companies from China to Russia to Africa make bold pronouncements about issues when it was clear that they didn't have any idea what they were talking about. But none of their people challenged them. Perhaps they believed what their managers were saying, or perhaps they couldn't admit that their leaders lacked the necessary knowledge. Whatever the reason, the managers' immaturity caused problems, since their companies sometimes based programs and policies on their false knowledge.

Flexibility is an essential component of learning maturity. There are times when people need to make adjustments to their routines and behaviors in order to learn. It might mean accepting a transfer to another group in order to learn. It might mean going from a glamorous position to a less glamorous one. It might require going back to school or signing up for training. It might involve a willingness to be coached and to respond to the coaching by trying new things. It might require people to be willing to fail as they tackle a challenging assignment—failure being the first step to learning a difficult lesson.

In some developing countries, however, flexibility as well as humility may be seen as signs of weakness—of being uncertain and fickle. The tribal leaders or royal personages or government rulers are esteemed for demonstrating steadfastness of purpose and action and for being confident and assertive. Thus, they may strike others in the culture as being true leaders, but they may also limit their ability to learn.

The Government Factor

Be aware, too, that in some developing countries, a large percentage of employees have spent a significant amount of time working for government-run businesses. As a result, they are accustomed to being told what to do and not accustomed to being asked for their ideas. This is especially true in current and former Communist countries where people labored within vast bureaucratic structures and felt like cogs in a machine; they were not expected to learn and grow.

In these instances, all three types of maturity are impacted. People who have worked for government-run companies tend to lack the opportunity and incentive to develop business savvy. They also aren't required to master skills necessary to achieve minimal competence, limiting their learning maturity. And within the buttoned-up government structure, most people don't enhance their emotional maturity—there is a set way of relating to direct reports and managers that provides little room for developing humility, self-confidence, and so on.

Francis Yuen, the CEO of Trane who has worked extensively in Asia, noted that when he first began working in that region of the world, most of the employees came from state-run companies or the government. Though he said that things are changing and that a number of Chinese start-ups more closely resemble their Western counterparts in terms of being innovative and flexible, the old Communist thinking of the past lingers on.

"A lot of them [employees] are coming from a state-owned company, where really the companies are more directive. They communicate that stuff is to be done in this way. Do this! But they don't give a lot of room for creativity."

Francis added that many employees in Asia have been indoctrinated in consensus-building approaches: "You always talk about the welfare of the entire so-called group. So there is still the groupthink in planning."

Francis made it clear that he believes that Chinese employees are eager to be involved and that they want to be asked about their ideas, but that it may not be as simple as in the West to facilitate that involvement and draw their ideas out of them.

If you find yourself managing a significant number of people who have come up through government-run businesses, therefore, you probably will need to be much more patient when it comes to issues such as creativity, learning, risk taking, and commitment. In their old positions they weren't rewarded for these behaviors (and may well have been discouraged from adopting them). Therefore, you need to give your people more time and more encouragement to practice behaviors that require a higher level of maturity.

Why Maturity Matters: Execution, Results, and Other Impacts

For instance, Gene was running a division of a software company in a large Asian city, and most of his employees were from the Asian country where the company was based. From the very beginning of his tenure, Gene had been impressed by the superior business education and intelligence of his people, especially his team of five direct reports. In fact, Gene found that they were far more efficient than the people who had worked for him in the West, and they were especially adept at listening to and following orders.

But as good as they were at taking orders and doing what they were told, they were not so good at demonstrating the initiative necessary to get things done on their own. Gene discovered this truth when he asked his team to organize a presentation to senior management that offered five alternatives to a current strategy that had fallen short of objectives. Because his team was so adept at carrying out orders, Gene assumed they would have no problem with this one. Instead, they struggled mightily, in large part because the assignment required them to communicate with people outside of their normal lines of communication and because they had to demonstrate creativity to complete the assignment. They realized they had to come up with concrete, viable recommendations from what they learned. Eventually, Gene had to hire an outside consultant to help them with the presentation because he determined they were incapable of handling it on their own.

In our interviews, we've found that execution and results are common problems in developing countries, and though there are a number of reasons for these problems, low human capital maturity is a primary one. In Gene's case, his people lacked the business savvy maturity and emotional maturity to get the presentation done; they weren't skilled at working the various networks in the company to acquire the information they needed. They also lacked the confidence and communication skills required to accomplish their task at the level that Gene expected.

A lack of learning maturity can also hamper a group's ability to generate results. People who refuse to stay current with technological changes or adopt new methods or procedures will lack the tools necessary to achieve results. Similarly, individuals who resist training or coaching will not grow and develop in ways that they can complete challenging assignments or achieve higher levels of performance.

In addition, we've found that in some developing countries people have a task rather than a results orientation. They focus on getting a specific job done by a specific time in a specific manner, but they don't think about how they can make an impact with their work or ensure that a project moves forward. They don't think about how they have to include Bill in marketing if they want to have any chance of getting the green light from management or that they must figure out a way in advance of a product launch to ensure that retailers will live up to their verbal promises to provide good shelf displays for the product.

We're not writing this to disparage any culture, since every group in every country is perfectly capable of increasing its maturity levels. The problem is that when you've never been matured through the culture, through educational systems, and through training, you're less likely to think in terms of how to get things done.

Of course, the negative effects of a lack of maturity aren't limited to poor execution and results. On a macro level, if your workforce is low on the maturity curve, morale is also likely to be low because people lack the savvy to grasp the reasons for budget cuts, changes in policy, and the like—they overreact because they lack the experience to understand why a given management action was taken. On a smaller scale, people's lack of maturity can produce counterproductive behaviors that range from arrogance to indifference. A lack of business savvy maturity combined with a lack of emotional maturity can cause people to think they know more than they actually do. A lack of learning maturity can cause people to plateau prematurely. There are infinite variations on this theme, but the good news is that where people are on the maturity curve can be assessed and upgraded. First, though, we want to give you a better understanding of why developing countries are particularly vulnerable to low human capital maturity levels.

Four Major Causes

In the West, we have formal and informal processes designed to mature people for jobs. In the majority of cases, employees have some degree of emotional maturity, are capable of learning, and enjoy some business smarts. Education, training, mentoring, job rotations, and other factors all facilitate the maturation of employees.

In developing countries, some of these processes don't exist or are implemented with a low degree of effectiveness. Unless you appreciate why and how this is so, you may start work as a manager in a developing country and assume your employees have roughly the same level of maturity as people you're used to working with in the West. The following explanations, though, will disabuse you of this notion:

• Educational gaps

While more people in developing countries than ever before are being educated in the West, these individuals tend to be among an elite group; most of them are members of the ruling or affluent class. Most managers we've talked to who run groups in places like Asia, India, the Middle East, and South America note that the majority of people they supervise lack a strong educational background, especially in business. This means that they may never have received a strong foundation in business principles, served an internship in a company, or had a mentor. They may also have missed out on the simulated experiences of working in an organizational setting that good business schools provide. While the educational system in the West may not be perfect, it does get the maturation process rolling. Without consistent exposure to this system, people are inherently less mature when they begin to work in businesses.

- Inconsistent or nonexistent training regimens

In this category, we're including workshops, seminars, in-company universities and courses, external executive development programs, coaching, and so on. While the quality of these training processes can vary, the cumulative effect often helps people move up the maturity curve. In developing countries, employees may never have had access to any of these opportunities, or they may have been involved in only one or two training regimens of questionable quality or only short duration.

- Hiring and promotion policies

While nepotism and other forms of favoritism exist everywhere, they are more prevalent in developing nations. In many instances, hiring and promotion policies have always been corrupted by these nonbusiness goals. In fact, in some countries it has been an accepted practice that you had to know someone to get hired or that you had to be in a certain tribe, religion, sect, or family to receive a promotion to a certain level in a company. While Western companies that open offices in developing nations don't subscribe to these practices, they still may influence hiring and promotion decisions among managers who were raised in these cultures. Consequently, people are brought into organizations and given positions of considerable influence even when they lack emotional maturity or a willingness to learn. In fact, we've seen an unusual number of relatively young people in positions of power because they had good connections. While young managers can be mature, they often lack the seasoning that catalyzes the maturation process.

- Immature business environments

Your people may have both experience and expertise, but they are still relatively low on the maturity curve. The problem is that they have been working in business environments that lack well-defined systems and processes. Essentially, they have been laboring in environments that have all the sophistication and formal structures of a mom-and-pop business. This isn't to say that they failed to acquire knowledge and skills working in these environments—they may have actually had the chance to move faster and do more without being hampered by bureaucratic red tape. As a result, they may appear to be mature—they clearly possess a number of years of experience working effectively in a given country—yet they have never worked as part of a team or in a functional structure or been charged with developing their direct reports. Thus, they are mature in certain ways, immature in others.

Assessment: Where Your People Are on the Curve

Admittedly, this assessment isn't easy to make initially. As we've noted, you can be misled by high levels of experience and expertise as well as by strong Western educational backgrounds. Similarly, you may have people who are highly mature in one area (business savvy maturity, for instance) and highly immature in another area (emotional maturity, for instance). Over time, though, you will probably develop a good sense of their maturity levels through observation.

Unfortunately, by then it may be too late. It can take months to determine where people are on the maturity curve—and the more people you're responsible for, the more time it takes to make this determination. To accelerate the assessment process, here are some questions to ask regarding maturity in each of our three areas:

Business Savvy Maturity

1. Have your people ever worked in a formal process before or have they operated in a business function? Have they learned to implement policies and programs, and do they have a sense of how what they do fits into the larger purpose of the group or the organization?
2. Have they ever worked as part of a team? Do they seem comfortable working with a diverse group of individuals, and can they deal with conflict and reach consensus in a team setting?
3. Do they have a sense of how to get things done? Have they ever been the point person on a project and were responsible for achieving an objective? Do they seem lost when they're asked to execute a plan or launch a program, or are they able to handle the assignment with relative skill?

Emotional Maturity

1. Does their ego get in the way of obtaining results, achieving consensus, or reaching a group goal (at the expense of an individual one)?
2. Are they able to handle workplace stress effectively? Can they deal with deadlines, crises, and other difficult situations without controlling or withdrawing?

3. Have they had previous work experiences in which they had to handle stressful situations in order to succeed? Do they admit to mistakes and failures and demonstrate that they've grown as a result of these experiences? Have they demonstrated an ability to function effectively in complex, ambiguous, or volatile situations?

Learning Maturity

1. Are they willing and able to acquire new knowledge and skills? Do they seem eager to tackle new assignments and challenging projects (or do they try to weasel out of them or avoid them in other ways)?
2. Have they demonstrated a history of learning new knowledge and skills over time? Have they been in jobs where they had to master a new area in order to succeed?
3. Are they adept at listening, absorbing, and adjusting, or are they unwilling to change no matter what people tell them? Do they demonstrate the flexibility necessary to move away from standard practice and adopt a new standard?

You can ask these questions of employees and people with whom they've worked as well as observe these individuals in action to arrive at a maturity rating. As you'll discover, this is not an exact science. For one thing, people won't always respond accurately to these questions, so you need to take their answers with a grain of salt. For another, people may prove to be very mature in one area, very immature in another, thus confusing you further. And if you're trying to determine where a larger group of people falls on the human capital maturity curve rather than only a few, then the task becomes even more challenging, in part because you'll probably have to rely on the observations of others rather than just your own.

These caveats aren't meant to discourage you from using these questions but to suggest that arriving at the right maturity rating may take a bit of time and patience. Ultimately, we've found that it's best to start out by targeting a small group—ideally, your direct reports. This will make the process manageable. In addition, think about maturity in terms of high, medium, and low in each category. This will help you differentiate between someone who seems incredibly mature in one area and someone whose maturity is just average or very low.

It also helps to rely on your experience and instinct in making a maturity determination. In most instances, if you're able to observe direct reports in action with these questions in mind and talk to them about some of the issues the questions raise, you'll be able to make a fairly accurate assessment in most cases.

To help you with this assessment, we'd like to share with you profiles of two managers who worked for a Western company in India. Anish and Shiva were both in their early thirties and had followed similar paths. Though Anish had grown up on the outskirts of Mumbai and Shiva near New Delhi, they had both attended two of the top business schools in India—Anish had received his degree from the Indian School of Management, and Shiva received his from the Faculty of Management Studies at the University of Delhi. Both had done supremely well in school as well as in their first jobs after graduating—Anish in Mumbai working for a large food-based distributor and Shiva in

Bangalore working for a high-tech firm. They each had worked at two other Indian firms before being hired by the Western company opening an office in Mumbai. Neither had ever worked anywhere but in India, and their trips to other countries had been relatively few and brief.

Their boss, Anne, who was from the United States, met both of them when she was transferred to Mumbai; Shiva had already been working there for eight months, and Anish had been there just over a year. Anne was immediately struck by Shiva's extraordinary business skills—his mind was quick as lightening, and he possessed an almost encyclopedic knowledge of the company's history, its products, and its failures and successes in recent years. He was also brilliant at analyzing the current strategy and its strengths and weaknesses. Anish was not quite as quick as Shiva nor did he have instant access to all the relevant facts and figures or the laser-like analytical ability that Shiva possessed. Still, he had a moderate degree of business savvy maturity.

Anne quickly discovered, however, that Shiva was extremely low in emotional maturity and low in learning maturity. Perhaps because Shiva had been raised in a Brahmin, highly affluent household or because school and work had always come so easy to him, he was impatient and intolerant. More than once, he spoke sharply to Anne when she asked him a question he clearly perceived to be dumb. She also noticed that he had difficulty getting along with some of his colleagues and that he often ate lunch by himself in the company cafeteria. Despite Shiva's intelligence and business savvy, he was also locked into a certain way of doing things. Like other people who are smart and successful, he had hit upon an approach that worked and stuck with it. As a result, he struggled with the transition to new systems and policies.

Anish, on the other hand, quickly proved to be at the middle or high level in his emotional and learning maturity. Gracious and with a good sense of humor, he was willing to say "I don't know" when he wasn't sure about what to do next on a project, and he was especially good relating to people at all levels in the organization. Anish also was hungry to learn new skills and frequently volunteered for assignments that would require him to stretch his capacities.

Anne also made a point of talking to other Indian colleagues about Anish and Shiva—she asked one of them if perhaps Shiva's manner was acceptable in Indian culture and that perhaps she was missing something. The person she asked responded, "He is a jerk in any culture." On the other hand, no one had a bad word to say about Anish except that he needed to build up certain competencies in order to fulfill his potential.

In this way, Anne was able to determine that Anish was higher on the human capital maturity curve than Shiva; she wasn't fooled by Shiva's business savvy into thinking that he possessed a degree of maturity he actually lacked.

Effective Responses to Maturity Levels

Once you've done your assessment, you're in a good position to manage human capital maturity effectively. Managing maturity can mean a number of things, from hiring/firing to training and coaching. We'll talk about the specifics of these responses in a moment, but first we want to warn you about a common mistake many Western leaders make when assessing maturity levels in developing countries.

Many times, we've seen smart, insightful Western leaders who ignore their own instincts and judgments when it comes to the maturity of their people. Just as Anne wondered if her opinion of Shiva might be off base because his behavior was acceptable within his culture, Western executives distrust their own opinions as culturally biased. In essence, they commit the opposite sin of the truly biased Western executive and suboptimize their own experiences. For example, they believe that Manuel's or Mei's difficulty adjusting to a Western business process won't be a problem and that even though an individual has never worked in a formal business system before, they should not judge them based on Western business standards. Yet, well-intentioned Western leaders feel guilty; they don't want to be Ugly Americans and impose their standards. For this reason, they tolerate low business savvy maturity levels much to their regret down the road.

Don't fall into this trap. While you don't want to be jingoistic and discount the impact of a foreign culture and its way of doing business, neither do you want to discount your own business experience. If you see a problem with maturity in any of the three categories, you need to act:

- Act sooner rather than later.

If you find that your people are low on the human capital maturity curve, you may be tempted to take a wait-and-see approach, in part because of the previous point about not wanting to impose your Western ideas on a foreign culture. You may also rationalize the situation to yourself. One of the leaders we talked to noted that he could not believe his eyes that his Russian employees were as immature emotionally and from a learning perspective as he thought. On more than one occasion, he had evidence that people were drinking on the job, that people regularly made up excuses to leave work early, that the arrogance and corruption of some of his people was so great that the culture itself was corrupted. But he kept telling himself "when in Rome . . ." and failed to take action to correct the situation. It reached the point that it was almost impossible to get any projects completed, and he ended up quitting in frustration.

Our advice, therefore, is to not let it reach this point. Whether it's one immature employee or hundreds, you need to address the situation as soon as you identify it. You have a window of opportunity to act in your early weeks and months on the job; people tend to be more open to your suggestions and directives during this honeymoon period. This is especially true in developing countries where people understand that you've been brought in precisely because you possess the Western business knowledge they may lack. If you wait too long to make changes, however, your actions may be seen as reactive and panicky rather than proactive and reasoned.

- Use the discomfort zone method.

Whether the people you target are struggling with maturity in business savvy, emotional, or learning areas, you need to structure a step-by-step program that pushes them to develop the maturity required. Like any development program in the West, you can choose from formal training, coaching/mentoring, job rotation, and challenging assignments, but you need to be sure that this program creates discomfort. In other words, to mature your people relatively quickly, they need to test behaviors and be given challenges they've never faced before. No doubt, some of them have never been pushed like this in previous jobs. Just about everyone experiences some degree of discomfort in these situations.

But this is the first litmus test. Some people won't want to mature; they will refuse to grow emotionally, to learn new things, to develop business savvy. They won't tolerate the discomfort. It's better to know this fact immediately; these individuals are incapable of becoming the type of employee you need.

On the other hand, some individuals will view the discomfort as a challenge. In fact, we've found that many people in developing countries handle the discomfort of change and growth better than people in the West. Many of them have dealt with discomfort all their lives—they've endured wars, famine, flood, and so on. They often have served in the military or been brought up in societies that frequently tested their abilities. Consequently, they understand the purpose of discomfort as a growth mechanism and respond to it positively.

- Make the training participatory and fun.

You're not going to help someone acquire business savvy or become more personally mature through dry lectures. A significant percentage of training in the West mimics the classroom teaching experience: an expert stands in front of a group and explains what it is they need to learn and do. Some of this is usually necessary, and people in the West are more responsive to this classroom approach than people in developing countries. More often than not, trainers find that when they lecture at length to employees in developing countries, people's eyes glaze over.

Rob learned this the hard way when he was conducting a training session in China for employees and managers trying to adapt a Western sales promotion to their country. The first few hours of the session involved Rob and other presenters talking and the employees listening. Based on the blank looks on their faces and the scant feedback, it seemed clear that they weren't engaged. He decided he needed to do something different to get them more involved in the process, otherwise they would not internalize the lessons that were being taught.

In the back of the room were several promotional items, and there was a box of clapping hands to illustrate another promotion. Rob passed out the fake hands—they actually clapped together like real hands and made a noise that sounded like applause—and told the participants that they should clap the hands together when they heard a speaker say something they liked.

The transformation in their attitude was immediate and dramatic. They not only offered vociferous clapping whenever a point struck them as important, but their attention became intense. They were no longer just going through the motions of listening politely but were thinking about what was said and were relating it to their own work situations.

The process had become fun and involving, and that created an environment much more likely to help them become more mature as employees.

- Hire people with high maturity potential.

It may be that some of the people you inherit simply aren't mature and lack the ability or willingness to become more mature. When you take over, you may need to fire some of them, and some may leave of their own volition. Ideally, you'll have the chance to hire new people, and when you do, make sure you test for maturity. One easy way of doing this is to use a variation of the nine questions listed above for the three areas of maturity.

Another way is to use the method McDonald's uses in selecting people for assignments in developing countries. Rich Floersch, McDonald's vice president of human resources, said that during the interview process people are tested based on three criteria: a proven track record (whether they can demonstrate the ability to produce results), adaptability (whether they have the capacity to be flexible and manage changing circumstances), and learning (whether they are willing and eager to learn).

From our perspective, this last criterion is key. You can use coaching and training to help individuals develop business savvy and to grow as individuals, but it's extremely difficult to teach someone to want to learn. Some employees in developing countries are content to have a job; they may have had the capacity to learn scared out of them, or they may have experienced such corruption in their country and companies that their cynicism stands in the way of their learning. For this reason, you want to get a sense of whether a candidate for a job seems eager to acquire new knowledge and skills. Pay attention to whether he or she speaks proudly of competencies acquired in a previous job—does the individual consider learning a real accomplishment?

Finally, we should point out the obvious: some companies in developing countries deal with a lack of human capital maturity by bringing in Western executives. This is an effective temporary solution, since it moves a company up on the human capital maturity curve. Ultimately, however, organizations want and need the native population to mature. If a developing country's management ranks are top-heavy with Western executives, they are akin to a colonial power. Employees need to have a significant number of their own people in positions of authority for them to respond with the greatest level of commitment and energy. In Dubai, Bob started out with a number of Western executives, but the goal was to transition these executives out of the organization eventually and replace them with Arab employees.

Generally, organizations in developing countries go through a transition process. They start out with numerous people and processes that are immature. Then Western executives come in and work with native leaders to help the processes and people become savvier. Gradually, at least some of the Western leaders depart and are replaced by native employees. The time frame for increases in maturity varies considerably from country to country and from company to company. Western leaders, though, need to be aware that as they help their people become more business savvy, more emotionally intelligent, and better able to learn, they may be thinning the ranks of Western executives. Ideally, your ability to achieve this objective will earn you kudos from the home organization as well as more tangible benefits. In fact, Western leaders who are adept at maturing organizations in developing countries increase their own value, not only to their own companies but on the open market since this is a highly prized skill.

CHAPTER 5

Become Attuned to the Shades of Yes

In the West, we like to think that a deal is a deal, that a contract sets things in stone, and that people can be counted on to follow through on what they say they'll do. While none of this is always true, most business executives operate as if these precepts are valid in the majority of situations they face. When our direct report tells us he'll have the white paper on our desk by Friday, we fully expect to see it by the end of the week. When a customer promises to give us a new piece of business, we trust that his word is his bond.

In developing countries, however, things aren't as cut-and-dried. It's not that people there are any less honest than we are—as we know from all the recent US financial and corporate scandals in the news, everyone from CEOs to consultants is capable of deceit. In fact, if anything, we're more devious in our dishonesty than individuals in developing countries. We know how to spin the truth so that later we can claim with all sincerity that we weren't lying on purpose. We are careful to make one pronouncement in public (in speeches, to the media) and say something else in private.

But in places like the Middle East, Asia, Africa, and South America, people are much more comfortable with ambiguity and uncertainty—saying that they agree or that they'll do something is merely a holding action before they make a real decision or a way to avoid the type of confrontation and conflict they dislike. They are more likely to say yes to be polite than to signal final agreement. The way they say yes—their body language and tone of voice—can have a lot more meaning than their actual words.

As a manager in a developing country, you're likely to find yourself in a variety of situations where people you work with will agree to deals, promise you delivery dates, and tell you that they're on board for a new project. In other words, they will say yes in a variety of ways and situations, and your success will depend on how well you read their yes.

We've found that this type of reading isn't easy for many neophyte managers in developing countries. It may not be easy, but it's essential, and we're going to suggest ways in which you can become skilled at interpreting the shades of yes.

Cultures that Encourage "Say-Do" Differences

Here are three quick stories that illustrate why, from a cultural perspective, it's acceptable to say one thing and do another.

When Bob worked in various parts of Asia, he sometimes had to make a purchase at a store (a television, stove, etc.) or get his phone or Internet installed. He would tell the salesperson, "I'd like it delivered (or installed) tomorrow" and ask if that would work. They would tell him that was fine. In fact, they had no intention of delivering it the next day. He learned that they weren't lying to him in order to make a sale or out of malice. Given their cultural framework, they simply didn't want to disappoint him. They didn't want to have a negative conversation, and the easiest way to avoid that was by telling him what they thought he wanted to hear.

In Dubai, Bob had two key employees—Nasib, an investor, and Sadad, an employee. Nasib was a Dubai financial guru, and Sadad was more involved in the day-to-day operations. During meetings, these two men were always polite to one another and made a point of saying yes to each other's projects and proposals. Behind the scenes, however, each man did his best to sabotage the other. Part of the cultural impetus for this sabotage was that each of them was seeking status in society, and each felt the other stood in his way—in a tribal society, win-lose scenarios are much more common than win-win ones. But more important, Nasib and Sadad were related—Sadad's wife was Nasib's niece. Before Bob arrived, Sadad had divorced his wife. In the West, this might not be a big deal, but it is a major problem in the Middle East. In that society, divorce has been rare. If a man becomes estranged from his wife, he simply gets another one—men are allowed up to four wives. Sadad's action was grievously offensive to Nasib and his family, creating the behind-the-scenes feud. To the casual observer at work, however, their willingness to support each other and agree to each other's requests made it seem like they were the best of colleagues.

In the West, their boss would have told them to sit down and work out their problems or they'd be gone, or the boss might bring in a coach to work with them. In Dubai, though, the situation was much more complex, and the way they handled it was by saying yes in public business situations and ignoring the yes in private.

These two stories are indicative of cultures where yes doesn't always mean yes—where it's permissible to signal agreement or make a promise while knowing that one might renege on it. While every country has its own idiosyncrasies when it comes to making commitments and communicating agreement, we've found that certain factors are common in many developing countries that cause yes to mean no, maybe, or probably (or something else entirely):

- Extended negotiation is the norm. Historically, tribes and religious groups in developing countries employ extended processes to reach decisions. From ceremonies in which people pray to gods to tribal meetings in which issues are debated for days or weeks, the process for reaching a firm decision takes time. In these countries, the expectation is that important decisions require discussion, reflection, and sometimes divine entreaties and signs. People there recognize that initial positions may not be final positions. Thus, they attach less importance to what people say and commit to at the beginning than when it's time for a final decision.

- Patience is a necessity. In developing countries, it often takes much longer to get something done than in the

West. Because of bureaucratic red tape, lack of resources, poor infrastructure, and volatile environments, citizens of these countries have learned to be patient. They understand that deadlines may come and go with no negative repercussions and that delays are inevitable. For these reasons, people may agree to delivering a report on a given day or to contacting a customer by a certain time, but they understand that no harm is done if it takes longer to accomplish these tasks than what they agreed to.

- Haggling is an art form. If you've ever been to a bazaar or market in a developing country, you have encountered a seller who started out by saying something like, "I will sell you this fine Persian rug for $50 dollars and not a penny less!" Of course, this is simply an opening gambit, and such merchants fully intend to sell it to you for less. But the gap between what they say and what they will do is the essence of haggling. They see nothing unethical in this tactic; it's just the way buying and selling is conducted. Consciously or not, this practice carries over to business situations. For instance, an employee may say he requires a certain salary increase, or he can no longer afford to work for the company, but he is simply using this statement as a bargaining device.

- Switching sides is a historical imperative. For hundreds of years, people in developing countries have survived by aligning themselves with the new party in power. It may be switching allegiance to a conquering nation or tribe or new form of government. Historically, changing outward loyalty has been a matter of survival. More recently, this type of switching has had a strong financial component—aligning oneself with the ruling powers or the most powerful local politician can result in jobs and other financially beneficial situations. Thus, when these individuals become corporate employees, they instinctively (and perhaps again, unconsciously) are alert to which way the wind is blowing. They are acutely aware of the benefits of doing what is politically expedient, and so they may say they are supporting one program in a meeting only to switch their support in the next meeting.

Translating Cultural Attitudes to Work Behaviors

Direct, impatient Western managers are often taken aback by the byzantine ways work is accomplished in developing countries. More than that, they can become flustered and frustrated by how direct reports, colleagues, bosses, customers, and suppliers fail to do what they say by when they say they will do it. They can't believe that someone would back out of a deal after they shook hands on it or that a promised budget never materializes, or they feel like they have to clean out their ears because they were sure a colleague said they had a deal, but later he claimed that he said that he thought a deal was possible. We've known some managers who simply could not handle the disconnect between what is said and what is done; they became so suspicious and paranoid that they couldn't function effectively or just quit.

If, however, you're aware of when and why people are likely to say yes when they mean something else, you will be able to handle the disconnect. For instance, many direct reports in developing countries will say yes or agree to a request because they want to avoid conflict. In the West, we encourage healthy debates; we want our people to disagree with us when they feel we're pursuing the wrong strategy, and more often than not, they are willing to do so. In developing countries, however, employees are often nonplussed when their bosses are overly direct in their questions or requests: "Do you have enough information to handle this assignment?" a manager might ask, and the blunt questions may cause the employee to say, "Sure." In fact, he may not be sure, but he thinks that his boss is counting on him to handle it, that there will be dire consequences if he expresses doubt, and so he says what he thinks the boss wants to hear. He doesn't want his boss to become upset about his lack of experience or cause a conflict around why he lacks the proper information.

Similarly, when you start working in a place like Saudi Arabia or China or South America, you may discover that at least with some projects it takes three times as long as in the West for people to reach consensus and take action. Perhaps you're having an initial meeting with a customer about a contract, or you're trying to get your team to agree on a new product strategy. At the initial meeting, it may seem like you're just about there—people seem to like the terms of the contract or the strategy you propose. No one dissents during the meeting, and you're confident that at the next meeting everything will be resolved and things will move forward.

In fact, you discover nothing has been resolved. People won't tell you that they think the contract is unacceptable in its present form, and they won't express dissatisfaction with elements of your strategy. Instead, they may follow a course of action that we in the West term passive-aggressive. To your face, they may say that they like everything proposed but just need more time to "study the situation." Behind the scenes, the customer may have his boss send you a suggestion that requires rewriting the contract. Or their resistance may come in dribs and drabs. In other words, at the next meeting they may raise a minor objection—something rather insignificant and easily changed—but at each subsequent meeting there is another objection, another change. Rather than tell you straight out that the entire contract must be rewritten, they try and make the changes more palatable by voicing their opposition slowly and subtly. They expect you to get the message, but it takes some Western managers a long time to figure out what is being communicated.

Earlier, we noted that haggling was part of the bazaar mentality that is common in many countries. Drawing out the negotiation is the equivalent of the lengthy give-and-take that precedes a sale in street markets. While street market haggling generally involves much more drama than occurs in organizations, the give-and-take, the prolongation of what is a relatively short process in the West, is the same.

We should also note that people in developing countries don't have the transaction mentality that dominates Western managerial thinking. By transaction mentality, we mean wanting to get the deal done as fast and as advantageously as possible. We see sales and deals in terms of winners and losers, in terms of starts and finishes. In many countries, however, people lack this transaction mentality. Instead, they see business interactions as opportunities to develop relationships as well as to get deals done. Much more so than people in the United States, for instance, people in these countries want to know the person they're going to do business with before they actually do any business. For this reason, they may say yes when they don't mean it because it buys them time to establish whether someone is smart and trustworthy. Obviously, a direct report will go about this process more carefully than a boss or a customer, but all of them won't give a final yes until they feel they know you and like what they've found out about you. They move on to transactions only after they feel a good relationship has developed.

What all this should be telling you is something we alluded to earlier in the chapter: Patience is a virtue in developing countries. We understand that if it's your first posting to somewhere halfway across the world, you want to make an impact immediately and show your bosses that you can handle the assignment. Consequently, you charge into a situation with both guns blazing, ready for action.

Patience, on the other hand, puts you in a much better position to deal with shades of yes. For one thing, it offers you the chance to assess the other person at the same time that he or she is assessing you. For example, Don worked for an oil company, and he was brought in to manage a production facility in a Middle Eastern country. Don had worked all over the Western world—the United States, France, Australia, Italy—and was confident in his ability to thrive in a foreign culture. The majority of people working for him were citizens of the Middle Eastern country, but they spoke English well, and most had MBAs. They were a smart and experienced group, but it was clear from the start that Don and his people were having problems. In their first meeting together, Don did almost all of the talking and asked few questions—he laid out his plan for the facility and the improvements he wanted made. All his people were very respectful and agreed with all his points. In the second meeting, Don was visibly frustrated with the slow progress being made on action points he had listed during the first meeting. He chewed out two of his people who had explicitly stated that they would have something for him to look at by now, and he threatened serious consequences if he didn't have the projects started and reports made by the time of the next meeting. Again, everyone in the room agreed that they would have what he wanted when he wanted it. And again, by the time of the third meeting, little progress had been made. Everyone offered reasonable excuses, but Don was furious. After that third meeting, Don met with his boss and told him what was going on. His boss, a veteran of managing in developing countries, laughed and told him, "As soon as you lose your patience, you lose your power."

Don's boss explained that just as he was eager to assess his people, his people were eager to assess him. They weren't about to do what he asked until they felt comfortable with him; they also didn't tell him that what he was proposing was unreasonable—they didn't want to upset him. His boss advised him to move more slowly, to listen more and talk less and allow his group to become comfortable with who he was as a person and as a manager.

It was great advice, and Don eventually was able to manage his transactional, get-it-done-now style and learned to work effectively with his people. But being patient is only one piece of good advice when it comes to dealing with the shades of yes. Let's look at other ways you can prepare yourself for all the positive responses you're bound to receive.

Five Ways to Test the Yes

One way or another, successful leaders in developing countries learn how to test the yes. In our conversations with people who have worked all over the world as well as in our own experience, we've found that managers create their own methods for determining what a yes means. As a result, we identified five tests that can help you evaluate what a yes really means:

   1. Observe how the yes is said.

Beware of the neutral yes, the response that feels perfunctory, merely polite, and unemotional. This neutral yes is often an indication that the speaker doesn't mean what he says. On the other hand, a strong, emphatic tone combined with add-ons—commitment dates relating to the yes, explanations of how the yes will be accomplished—signify a sincere desire to follow through on what is promised.

   2. Ask follow-up questions that reveal an individual's thinking on the matter at hand.

This is a bit tricky in that most Western leaders either tend to grill their subjects or ask questions designed to elicit yes-or-no answers. In the former case, grilling people will only result in them telling you what they think you want to hear, not what they really believe or will do. In the latter case, they simply reiterate their initial response. Your goal for follow-ups is to encourage people to express what's really on their minds. For example, if you hear a neutral yes in response to your request that your people attend a trade conference next month, you might ask, "What do you think of these trade conferences?"

or "What would you hope to get accomplished if you attend the conference?"

There's no guarantee that they'll be up-front with you, but at least you give them the opportunity to raise issues that might affect their yes and that otherwise would be hidden from view. The odds are that you can anticipate issues and problems that might concern them regarding a particular issue. If a colleague offers you a neutral yes about participating on a particular team, ask him about his experiences participating on teams at the company in the past. If a customer gives you a neutral yes about giving you a big order for its new division, ask about the issues he envisions that might help or hinder the launch of the new division.

3. Push to determine if people have an action plan or execution strategy.

In other words, assess what specifically your people plan to do to make their yes happen. Will they provide you with an amended or signed contract by a certain date? How do they plan to approach a supplier with the changes you want them to make? What do they plan to do in order to enact a new internal policy and when will they do it?

The more detail they provide about how they will do what they say, the more likely it is that they're sincere about doing it. On the other hand, if they offer vague or no specifics about their plans for taking action, then it's likely their yes is only a maybe or a no.

4. Suggest a worst–case scenario.

Posing a hypothetical crisis or other type of problem can provide people with the opportunity to express their reservations about a plan or policy. What you're testing is their willingness to follow through on a commitment if circumstances change. Ask a question that starts, "What would you do if…?" More specifically: "What would you do if our workers went on strike?" Or: "What would you do if we had another fire in the plant?" Or: "What would you do if those rumors of a government collapse came to pass?" You want to bring their unstated concerns to the surface and discuss them. Even if those fears seem far-fetched and paranoid to you, they may be very real to the individual you're dealing with. In fact, worst-case scenarios that may never happen in the West can be common in developing countries. You may not have a clue of what can go wrong because you're new to the area, so asking these types of questions about worst-case scenarios not only tests the yes but alerts you to issues you might not be aware of.

5. Create and compare takeaways.

Early on in Dubai, Bob held a meeting at the end of which he was convinced that everyone in the room had agreed to a contract. Later, though, when he asked members of his team what they thought the outcome of the meeting was, he realized that his interpretation was significantly different from theirs. From that point on, he instituted a policy of comparing takeaways.

On one level, this means having discussions with key members of a team about what they got out of the meeting— for example, did they all agree that José wanted to collaborate with their company on the new project? But comparing takeaways shouldn't stop there. The key information to be gleaned involves expectations versus realities. In other words, prior to a meeting, figure out what you expect from an individual or individuals. If you decide to give a direct report a project that will require a tremendous amount of time and effort, do you expect him to protest, to ask a lot of questions, or to embrace it enthusiastically? If there's a gap between your expectations and the reality, then that's a red flag. If he says he is excited about getting to work on it but you were sure that he would feel intimidated by it, you need to talk with him and ascertain what he's really thinking.

In developing countries, this gap between expectations and realities appears more often than in the West. Again, this is because you may not have a good understanding of the experiences and issues your people are dealing with. You aren't aware that they may have had a horrible experience working on a similar project in the past or that they come from a culture where expressing anything less than unrestrained enthusiasm for a new assignment is considered bad etiquette. Whatever the cause of the gap between expectation and reality, investigate it when it appears—especially when people say yes.

Situational Strategies

Testing the yes takes time. You're not going to be able to ascertain what a yes really means in one quick meeting. Implementing the five tactics listed above can require a series of meetings or one-on-one conversations over an extended period of time. Similarly, you need to give others a chance to work through whatever issues they have regarding their affirmative response. This is true when you are trying to get your direct report to carry out a specific task, but it's especially true when more complex issues are involved—for example, when you're trying to form a partnership with an outside company or when you're trying to finalize a budget. If you're dealing with individuals you have no positional authority over, you lack the clout to enforce the yes they've given you, and so you're going to need additional days or weeks to coax them into doing what they said they would do.

In addition, think about final approval as requiring a series of steps. Obtaining a real yes happens in stages. In the West, you might schedule a budget meeting to approve the new numbers. In a developing country, you probably will have to set a number of interim steps after gaining initial agreement on that budget: a meeting one week later to review previous decisions and reach agreement on one budget item, another meeting two weeks later to address problems caused by budget item number 5, and another meeting three weeks later to achieve consensus on making changes to budget item number 4.

You'll find that people tend to be more amenable to saying yes and sticking to it when they're confronting small pieces of the larger whole. You'll get approval on the larger whole eventually, but you have to approach it piece by piece. There are all sorts of questions and concerns in developing countries that might prevent someone from providing a firm yes—for example, the need to speak with a government official about the matter at hand, to find a way to make the amount of work required manageable—and the bigger the issue at stake, the more likely these questions and concerns are to emerge. Smaller decisions tend to raise fewer obstacles to a decisive yes.

In addition, creating gaps between "affirming" meetings fits with the way work is done in many foreign cultures. These cultures recognize the value of digesting information, talking with others about it, and engaging in reflection. They say yes, and then they discuss and think about the implications of that yes. In this way, they come to conclusions they're comfortable with and can eventually reach a point where they are fully supportive of what they agreed to initially.

Dennis, who managed global supply chains in a variety of developing countries and also was a top executive in the Middle East, provides another perspective on getting to the yes slowly. His experience has taught him that in some developing countries it's a mistake to ask for a yes too quickly. He found that even if people say yes in response to your insistent demand for closure, it's likely to result in a no later.

"In a US-oriented managing style, we pride ourselves on bringing things to a decision quickly and being decisive and having press meetings around data," Dennis said. "Instead, we need to take time to build relationships and understand people's various viewpoints, both in meetings and outside of meetings."

Dennis proposed the following situational strategy to use when you believe that your proposal is going to meet with resistance, despite the positive initial responses you expect you'll receive. He said that a way to kick off the process is to have an educational briefing rather than a meeting to make a decision. Next, follow up with one-on-one sessions with individuals who attended the briefing, seeking to understand their concerns. Then reconvene the group that attended the briefing and discuss the concerns, addressing what you'll do about them, and see if you have consensus around your proposed actions.

"If you have a majority or some momentum behind a motion to move it forward, that's the point where you should seek a decision and take it forward." We should also note another situation that arises in some countries: When people say yes, they expect something in return. Certainly, quid pro quo exists in the West, but in many developing nations it's a much more integral part of how business is done. This is true not just for business deals among equals but for relationships between managers and direct reports. Please don't misunderstand what we're communicating here. It's not that you have to promise a direct report a promotion if he gets you a report on time. The relationship between what you do for him and what he does for you is more subtle than that. But a nuanced give-and-take is often present when one person agrees to provide the other person with labor, support, resources, and so on. Therefore, it behooves you to discover what the other person wants in return for his solid yes. Investigate what type of work he enjoys doing the most or if there's a team or committee he wants to be on, or if he has an interest in going back to school or attending a workshop. You don't have to promise anything in return for his yes, but you should certainly raise the issue of his wants/goals and make it clear to him that you'll do what you can to help him achieve them. By doing so, you can turn a yes that means maybe into a yes that means yes.

The Advantages of Learning to Let the Yes Evolve

While some of you may find doing business in developing countries frustrating and inefficient, you may come to appreciate the benefits of a gestalt involving shades of yes. Sometimes, slower is better. Once you realize that the words,

"Yes, I agree," are nothing more than a placeholder, you don't get thrown when you discover two weeks later that the person didn't agree with you at all. In fact, you discover that using these verbal placeholders provides everyone with the time to understand an issue in depth, spot the problems, and refine the way a policy or program is implemented.

In the West, we generally try to reach decisions and take action as quickly as possible. While this can be necessary in some circumstances, it can also result in a rush to judgment and a lack of buy-in from involved parties. Many companies in the United States try to be the first to market or early adopters of the latest technology, only to be victimized by their lack of due diligence—taking more time would have resulted in a more well thought-out strategy or avoided the glitches that often come with cutting-edge technology. On a smaller scale, we've seen managers issue preemptive orders that cause direct reports to act before they've thought through what they're doing or have been convinced that what they're doing is the right thing. In these situations, people do what they're told without demonstrating much enthusiasm or initiative for their tasks.

In developing countries, the process of getting a yes from a group is often a slower, evolutionary process. Tom, for instance, was a senior vice president who had started working for a transportation company's Southeast Asian office. At one of his first meetings, he talked to his group about switching to new software for tracking shipped merchandise that Tom felt was far more effective than the software they were using. He demonstrated the new software to the group, and everyone agreed that it seemed superior to the old software. Tom said he was glad that they all thought the switch was the right move and that they would begin the change next month. He asked that in the interim, they begin practicing with the new software and introduce it to their people. Two weeks later at the next meeting, Tom asked the group what they thought of the software. Again, he received positive feedback. This time, though, when Tom asked more specific questions about aspects of the program or how employees were responding to it, Tom heard a lot of excuses and evasions: People were very busy, they hadn't had a chance to introduce the software to their people, they intended to get to it first thing next week.

Fortunately, Tom recognized that their yes wasn't really yes and began talking individually with some of his team members about the situation. He discovered that before he joined the company, the manufacturing VP had insisted on changing software and it had resulted in huge problems that had created all sorts of headaches. In addition, Tom was suggesting they use software from a company they were not familiar with, but they had a great deal of trust in the software manufactured by another company.

Tom recognized his mistake and began to introduce the new software gradually to his group. He had a software company representative come in and talk about and demonstrate the new software. He scheduled a series of one-on-one meetings allowing members of his team to express their concerns. He had the one manager in his group who was enthusiastic about the new software start using it with one of his customers and then had him share his positive experience with the larger group. It took a few months longer than Tom had expected, but he finally received a true commitment to the new software from all members of his group. Even better, the process resulted in members of his team making suggestions to the software company that helped them tinker with the software design and improved its usability for their shipping purposes.

One benefit, then, of adjusting to the shades of yes is that you foster engagement on the part of your people. In the West, we frequently make decisions and assign tasks in isolation. As much as managers like to think of themselves as bringing people into the decision-making process, the demands of deadlines and other pressures cause them to issue orders and assign tasks without consulting others. They may sincerely want to be inclusive, but they end up excluding many if not all of their direct reports.

In a culture that has shades of yes, however, you need to secure real buy-in to actions you want people to take. This means you have to expend more time and effort in discussing issues, requesting input, exploring potential problems, and following up on assignments. While this can feel like a hassle at first, it's also a great way to engage people. There is a universal desire for inclusion and engagement, but we've found it's more likely to happen in a developing country than a Western one. That's because good managers make the effort to test and tease out the yes. They solicit opinions and ideas and draw people into the work. When employees feel like their questions are being answered and their concerns are being heard, they have a vested interest in the outcome.

This leads us to the second benefit. To follow up on that initial yes response, you need to engage in more conversations with people than you ordinarily would in the West. As we noted in previous chapters, this is especially important to many employees in developing countries. They want their managers not just to appreciate their abilities but to know them as individuals. In a developing country, you have to be more of a networker. You have to ask your people more questions about their goals and problems (rather than just having them ask you questions). You need to gain their trust and listen hard to discover why they may be hesitant about an assignment you've given them or about providing you with a resource you requested. In fact, these follow-up conversations need to be conducted not just with direct reports but with other colleagues in the company as well as bosses, customers, and suppliers. You can expect a lot of initial yes responses from all of them, but you can also expect that these responses don't mean much until you test them and unearth what lies beneath them. This process takes time, but it will help you build relationships that will serve you well down the line. When people get to know you better and you get to know them, you may find that you can anticipate issues that lead to a nonbinding yes. After working there for a period of time, you can get to yes faster and more definitively.

Until then, though, resolve to take your time and make the effort to interpret what colleagues' stated approvals and agreements really mean.

CHAPTER 6

Help Others Save Face

Defined in broad terms, saving face involves maintaining other people's honor and respect in the eyes of their peers. To lose face is to lose one's self-esteem relative to other people. While employees in the West have their own sense of saving face, it tends to be a much less significant factor than in developing countries. In the West, people may experience wounded egos or feel that they've been unfairly criticized by their boss in a team meeting, but in most instances they can get past this loss of face with minimal impact on their work performance. In the United States and other Western countries, we've been told that we need to develop a thick skin, that we must solicit and learn from tough feedback, and that we have to put our egos aside in order to acknowledge our weaknesses and address them.

In developing countries, one's honor relative to others is a much more important issue. In fact, Asian countries, such as Japan, have a history of shamed leaders committing hara-kiri because of a loss of face. Even in modern times, there have been instances of business executives who have been shamed because of unethical business conduct and then committed suicide. In a number of these countries, status is more clearly delineated than in the West—castes, religious sects, and royal families all confer a definite hierarchical ranking on individuals via titles or other means. Thus, a heightened importance is attached to one's ranking, and a loss of face in a business situation is viewed as a personal as well as a professional failure. In fact, criticisms and other negative communications are handled much more delicately in these countries than in the West. A boss in the United States usually isn't shy about telling a direct report in front of others that he came up short on a task. In a developing country, this message tends to be conveyed through suggestion and inference, and it tends to be delivered one-on-one rather than in a group. As a result, face is often preserved.

In the past when the United States was a developing country, saving face was far more important than it is today. In the class-conscious, royalty-dominated Europe of the past, saving face was also an issue. A perceived insult in front of one's peers often resulted in a demand for a duel. Fortunately, duels were relatively infrequent because people were aware that they caused others to lose face at their own peril—it might result in a life-or-death situation. Though our societies have changed in ways that have diminished the importance of saving face, the same is not true in many other countries.

While definitions of saving face vary somewhat from one country to the next (we'll explore one significant variation a bit later), the lesson for Western leaders is the same: Be conscious of how important self-respect and honor are to your people and do what is necessary to preserve it.

Why Saving Face Matters in Business

Andrew had spent most of his working life as a manager with top US companies and their European divisions. He considered himself well-traveled and had vacationed in out-of-the-way places such as Thailand, Nepal, and Bolivia. When his company asked him to open a manufacturing facility in China, he readily accepted the assignment. At first, things went well as Andrew moved back and forth between company headquarters in the United States and the province in southwest China where the facility was to be located. While hiring employees and supervising construction of the facility during this time, Andrew worked closely with a Chinese native who had been educated in London and was also employed by the company—this individual would become Andrew's second-in-command.

When the facility officially opened, Andrew took up permanent residence there. In the initial months of the facility's operation, a number of relatively minor problems arose—a machinery issue, a flooding problem because of the rains, and so on. Though everything was moving forward and Andrew was feeling only moderate pressure from his bosses in the United States to get the facility operating at maximum capacity, he found himself being short with his staff. He knew he was demanding a lot, but he made an effort to balance his demands with praise. Though he was critical of those people he felt weren't pulling their weight or who had made mistakes, he would also compliment his staff when they did things right. Essentially, Andrew was maintaining the same management style that had served him well in the West.

He noticed, however, that a number of his people seemed unusually glum and quiet when they met with him. In meetings, they delivered their reports in a monotone and when they spoke, their eyes were often downcast. The longer this went on, the more it bothered him. When one of his key managers abruptly resigned, Andrew met with his senior vice president—the Chinese native who had been educated in London. Though this executive was reluctant to level with him, Andrew told him it was critical that he do so, since he sensed that he was hurting morale and, more important, preventing productivity from rising to an acceptable level.

Andrew's second-in-command reluctantly told him that he had committed three errors that had caused people to lose face:

- Becoming angry at individuals when they were surrounded by their colleagues.
- Being critical of employees without cushioning the criticism in any way (softening his language, pointing out good things they had done, etc.)
- Talking about how "he had done a task successfully" in the past and asking why a given employee hadn't done it that way.

Andrew was shocked that these actions had resulted in a loss of face, but he took his senior vice president's comments seriously and worked hard at repairing the damage. He was highly conscious of his temper and refused to let it get the better of him—he stopped any public displays of anger directed at employees when others were around. He also learned how to point out mistakes in a face-saving way—he was careful to explain that a mistake was common and that many people had made mistakes, or he turned his criticism into a positive: "Here is how you can do an even better job next time." And Andrew stopped talking about all the things he had accomplished and asking others to do as he had done—he had merely wanted to provide his people with an example of how to do a task the right way. Still, he recognized that he made employees feel as if they didn't measure up when he came across as being boastful.

Over time, Andrew's face-saving moves paid off. He noticed that the glum and quiet demeanors gradually became more animated. People started making eye contact with him when they came into his office for a meeting. He saw smiles and heard laughter when he engaged in conversations with at least some of his employees. And over time, the facility's workforce got its act together and productivity improved.

So saving face, as well as building face, counts. We've heard American managers say, "I don't care how my people feel; I just care if they can do the job." In these developing countries, however, when people feel they've lost respect or are shamed, they lose value as employees.

What You Say and What You Do

Face is a tricky concept for Western executives since we don't typically worry whether our remarks to a direct report cause him to lose his standing among his peers. In other words, we're not conscious of how we might cause someone to lose face. Just as significantly, we're not particularly aware about the nuances of saving face. It may seem that if you choose one person over another for a promotion, the "loser" will lose face. In fact, that's not necessarily so—it just depends on how the news of this decision is delivered.

To get a better handle on what face is—and what it isn't—let's look at four rules of face:

• Face is generally lost in a group setting.

While face can be lost in a one-on-one interaction—for example, the boss tells a direct report that he has been removed from a key team, and the direct report imagines the pitying stares of his former team members—it usually becomes an issue because other people are observing the interaction. Many times, people in developing countries can tolerate criticism or decisions that affect them negatively as long as they're communicated in private. It's only when this criticism is communicated in the presence of peers that people feel ashamed, humiliated, and worthless. Obviously, then, managers in these countries need to be careful about what they say or do when others are present.

• Face depends on what's important in an individual's culture.

In Dubai, Tariq was a Dubai Aerospace executive who was well-connected with the royal family but lacked the business skills necessary to handle his high-level job effectively. When Bob discovered that Tariq couldn't handle certain assignments, he began taking away various responsibilities from him. Interestingly, Tariq accepted the loss of responsibility, but he fought to keep his title, his secretary, and his office. In his culture, these outer trappings of success were what constituted face. Few people would be aware that his responsibilities had diminished as long as the veneer of success remained.

While face can relate to more substantive issues, it can revolve around appearances rather than realities. As strange as it may seem, taking away an employee's parking space may result in a greater loss of face than reducing his salary—it's the high visibility of the former that counts.

- Face is often a matter of how something is said or done, not what is said or done.

A harsh or raised tone of voice, a belittling look or gesture, a negative comment that is highlighted by the situation—all of these communication styles can have a devastating impact on people in developing nations. It's not a question of them being soft or unable to tolerate criticism. It's that in their society, when a person in authority deliberately causes them to lose face, it means they have done something shameful. A Western manager have may have good intent—he wants to help his direct report learn from a mistake—but his curt, dismissive rebuke comes across as a shaming action.

This rule is a tough one for many Western managers to abide by. They are accustomed to speaking "naturally." They don't measure their words or soften their tone when speaking to direct reports. They don't think about how chewing out someone in front of his peers might impact his stature relative to those peers. They just react. They pay much more attention to the specifics of what they say or do rather than to the way they say or do it. Consider, though, that in developing countries, employees may not understand every word spoken by the Western manager, but they grasp every gesture and tonal change.

- Face can vary based on culture.

As we noted earlier, the issues that affect status in one culture may be somewhat different in another culture. In one culture, for instance, not looking directly at someone when you're referring to him may be a gross insult, but in another culture a direct stare may carry a negative connotation. Our purpose here is not to run through the hundreds of variations since you're going to have to determine what constitutes face in a given country based on research and conversations with knowledgeable citizens of that country.

We do, however, want to make you aware of two broad distinctions regarding face that we've observed. In the Far East, saving face is the priority while in the Middle East creating bigger face is what matters. More specifically, in countries like Dubai, Saudi Arabia, Kuwait, and Jordan, there is a clear pecking order. As we've mentioned, in Dubai, license plate numbers indicate the relative power of an individual based on his relationship to the sheikh. People in these countries want to increase their rank, and anything that prevents them from doing so is of greatest concern to them. In the Far East, on the other hand, people are focused on anything that might take away the face they already have. Far Eastern cultures are much more polite and circumspect than those in the Middle East, and people in the former region are acutely sensitive to anything that makes them feel ashamed or "less than" they were before. It's not that people in the Middle East don't care about losing face or that people in the Far East don't care about creating bigger face. Our point is that the emphasis is different in each culture.

Jeff Johnson, who was the CFO for Toshiba USA for a number of years, shared some fascinating insights with us about saving face in that country. He makes the point that in Japan, face has many facets. In other words, it manifests itself in different ways in different areas of life. For instance, Jeff noted that respect was always given to a presenter and that no one would ever criticize that presenter as someone might in the West—to do so would cause a serious loss of face.

He also explained that age has a significant impact on face—the older you are, the more respect you receive. In the Japanese culture, older employees usually have more face than younger ones. In the United States, a young fast-tracker may have no compunction about challenging a veteran manager, but that would not happen in Japanese companies.

Jeff also said another aspect of face was helping bosses meet their objectives. "If our president took a position—he told his boss that he would make a $3 million profit on a product—then we would always want to help him save face in this situation. The finance team would make sure in any way that we possibly could that he would achieve that challenge to save his face."

We should also note that in some cultures, face has to do with respecting what's important to the people in that culture. Reckard Hedeby, who has been a CEO in Central America as well as in other parts of the world, found that in Costa Rica, "there is a big component of face in the way you deal with employees, and you have to learn how to have constructive discussions with them without them losing face."

Reckard explained that Costa Rica has a wait-and-see culture; people there don't immediately jump on board when a Western executive makes changes but first want to see evidence that something is working. He explained that if Western leaders respect this wait-and-see mind-set, employees will feel more empowered and be much more effective contributors.

The Wise Old Man Paradigm

Our first and best piece of advice when it comes to saving face is that you should adopt the Wise Old Man (WOM) approach practiced by many leaders in developing nations. In tribal, royal, and religious cultures, WOMs are often the managers of face. Whether they're tribal elders, shamans, or senior religious figures, they are masters at helping their people save face and build face (and they may also deliberately cause someone to lose face for a particular purpose). Most important, WOMs are highly conscious of face in all social interactions, and Western managers can learn a lot from their examples. Here are three key lessons:

- Avoid winner-loser outcomes.

In the West, we like to put two people in a figurative ring and say, "Let the best man win." Whether it's the competition for a promotion or a decision about who should receive a plum assignment, we accept that someone has to win and someone has to lose. We have a culture where the loser is supposed to accept his loss graciously, learn from it, and use the knowledge gained to do better next time. Regardless of whether losers always respond in this gracious and educational manner, it softens the blow of losing sufficiently so that we usually don't feel shame or a loss in stature.

The Wise Old Man approach, though, is very different. First, the WOM never puts the winner and loser in the same room together; he doesn't announce to both of them (or to others) who won and thus avoids shaming one in front of the other. Instead, he deals with each person one-on-one and delivers a message that makes the situation palatable to both.

In Dubai, the sheikh embodied the wisdom of elders, and Bob experienced his face-saving skills firsthand on a number of occasions. Once, he was meeting with the sheikh during a particularly frustrating part of his tenure, and Bob in a moment of pique, said, "I've had just about enough of this crap." Bob had not meant to use such strong language in the sheikh's presence, but the word just popped out. The sheikh's eyes grew large, and he communicated his concern and asked for more details. Bob explained that a few members of the sheikh's inner circle who were working with Dubai Aerospace had been creating a lot of problems for him and were preventing progress from being made. The sheikh asked who specifically was causing these problems, and Bob said he preferred not to talk behind their backs; he suggested to the sheikh that he invite them all for a meeting so he could air his grievances in their presence.

The sheikh seemed horrified at this possibility. Instead, he asked Bob to specify exactly what the problem was with each person and offered to talk one-on-one with each individual and help each one understand what he had to do differently in the future. The sheikh explained that he would not directly criticize them, but that he would alert them to the changes he wanted "indirectly, within the context of your [Bob's] concerns."

In this way, no one felt as if he were losing face or being denied the opportunity to develop more face. The sheikh used his authority to communicate what had to change, but he did so in a roundabout way, avoiding insulting anyone or making any accusations.

In the West, when you select a given individual for a promotion, there's often a second and even third candidate who wasn't selected. Typically, a manager will go to the individual not selected and tell him or her that there will be other opportunities in the future and that he or she should work on developing specific skills to position himself or herself for these opportunities.

In a developing country, however, you need to be more subtle in your approach. The aforementioned statement will make an employee feel like a loser. Instead, compensate the candidate who was not selected in some way. Provide her with a bigger office. Offer her an assignment that provides high visibility within the organization. And instead of saying she has to work on specific skills, put her in situations where she can learn these skills without criticizing her lack of them.

- Use recognition to increase face.

It's not just about helping people save face but about providing opportunities for them to develop more face. Raising the profile of your people through gestures, assignments, and other means is well within your power. Assuming you have been given a title and a mandate that demonstrates that you are a wise Western executive, you can use your stature to increase that of others. In this way, you can ensure that your key direct reports are loyal and productive.

In developing countries, a wise manager can communicate that a given individual is favored even with small gestures. In many instances, they don't formally say, "This is my favorite," but instead they communicate it in other ways. Here is another story about the sheikh that illustrates how this can be done.

One time Bob was summoned to attend an event in the middle of the desert in Dubai; he was told that the sheikh expected to see him there but was not told why. Bob drove to the event, got out of the car, and began walking around in the 110 degree heat, not sure where the sheikh was or what he was supposed to do. Suddenly, a caravan of cars roared up to the tents that had been set up. A number of prominent members of the royal family emerged from these cars, walking in formation like geese flying in a wedge. The sheikh, of course, was in the front of the wedge, and the sheikh stopped the procession when he came upon Bob. He greeted Bob warmly and told him how happy he was with the job he was doing and how well the business was growing. As the sheikh talked, the wedge behind the sheikh gathered in a circle about them, listening intently. To Bob, it was like a staged performance. Shortly thereafter, Bob discovered that as result of this performance, his requests were responded to with much greater speed than in the past, and the attitude of just about everyone he dealt with had changed—people were much more eager to do his bidding. In essence, the sheikh used that desert meeting to transfer power to Bob.

You won't have the same authority as the sheikh, but your Wise Old Man status is a valuable tool to build loyalty and increase productivity. To that end, consider the range of recognition tools at your disposal:

- greeting people warmly and offering compliments in group settings,
- providing impressive-sounding titles,
- taking people out to dinner, asking them to join you for cocktails, or engaging with them in other social activities that confer special status,
- giving them a bigger office or a corner office,
- providing select employees with secretaries or assistants, and
- providing them with parking spots or choice parking locations.

Some of these tools may seem like small things, but they're not considered small in developing countries. In fact, the more visible a perk is, the more likely it is to build face. In part, its face-building value is its visibility (as opposed to a raise, which is invisible). But the value is also due to how quickly word gets around that a given employee has received a bigger office or was invited out to dinner by the boss. Unlike employees in the West, people in developing countries are not shy about letting their colleagues know about their choice parking spot or their new administrative assistant. They aren't worried that others will be jealous or that they might invite resentment. Instead, they make sure to spread the word about whatever recognition they have received, knowing it will help them build face.

Recognition is a powerful motivator, so use it wisely. As a Wise Old Man, you don't want to overuse it and dilute its value. Ideally, you'll rely on it for strategic purposes, such as when you want to help build the stature of an employee who is essential for the group's or company's success.

- Rely on patience and silence.

It may seem as though Wise Old Men should be dispensers of wisdom, but in many cultures—Buddhist, Hindu, American Indian—the WOMs often demonstrate astonishing patience when listening to an individual's complaints or concerns and don't rush to fix things or offer advice. Instead, they keep their counsel, wait for events to develop, and only then offer a remedy.

Patience and silence are especially useful when it comes to preserving face. Too often, Western managers in developing countries disrespect their people inadvertently because they blurt out something during a conversation or jump on someone before they have had time to explain themselves or finish a project. Patience and silence preserve face, but impatience and saying the first thing on your mind can diminish face. While there are times when you need to push people to meet a deadline or need to communicate in order to correct a problem, it's wise to rely on patience and silence, at least at the beginning of your tenure in a developing nation. Get to know your people, your company, and your new country's customs and culture. Then you'll be in a better position to know when it's okay to speak your mind and when silence is called for.

- Save face up and down, good and bad.

Dennis, the global supply chain manager who you met in the previous chapter, found that face matters not just horizontally but vertically and when things go well and when they don't. As important as it is for employees to maintain face in front of their peers, in certain cultures they also want to save it in front of bosses and direct reports. He found that if he could help someone look good in the eyes of his boss (i.e., a customer and his boss), he earned a chit that could be cashed in at a later date. He said that sometimes helping people look good was nothing more than giving them credit for a decision that had already been made and had worked out successfully.

Similarly, Dennis learned that it was equally valuable to absorb some or all of the responsibility when things went wrong, protecting subordinates from the wrath of a boss. As he explained, "You have to realize it's a long game that you're playing for, versus a short game, in dealing with some of these different cultures overseas."

Therefore, look around (and up and down) for opportunities to save face. In fact, we've found that when Western leaders step up and take responsibility when a failure occurs or a mistake is made, the individual who is shielded by this action is enormously grateful. Sometimes, employees in developing countries are not accustomed to a boss stepping up in this way. It is unexpected, and as a result it will be remembered. By saving face now, you may benefit a month or even a year from now. As Dennis noted, if you're in it for the long haul, saving face in this way will help you. It will earn loyalty, extra effort, and a willingness to provide you with inside information (about the company and the country) that can make a difference in your effectiveness. Spreading the credit around builds face, but when a Western leader protects a subordinate from losing face, that probably has even greater value.

Warning Signs

In some instances, you may cause one of your people to lose face. This isn't your intent, but you say or do something that you think is innocuous but that causes an employee shame or embarrassment. When this happens, you need to respond quickly and try to give face back, using the suggestions in the previous section. Many times, you can compensate for your mistake with an immediate response; the more time passes, the more the person feels the loss of face.

You may not be aware that you've caused a loss of face since people don't respond to your words and deeds as they might in the West. They don't become overly defensive or angry. In fact, if you're stressed out and busy, you may notice nothing amiss. Therefore, you need to be alert for the following signs of a loss of face:

- Silence

While Wise Old Men may use silence as a face-saving tool, it can also be a warning sign that someone feels disrespected or ashamed. In Taiwan and other Asian countries, a mute response is a very common sign that a loss of face has occurred. Jack, for instance, was a manager working in a food company in Taiwan, and he was talking to a direct report who had failed to inform him about a meeting scheduled with a supplier. He was careful to speak calmly, even though he was a bit peeved that his direct report hadn't told him about the meeting. Jack insists that he didn't rebuke his direct report but communicated that he wanted to receive regular emails updating him on all scheduled supplier meetings. Jack added that the direct report didn't offer an explanation of why Jack wasn't informed nor did he seem upset about what Jack was telling him. He simply nodded at appropriate moments, took some notes, and then departed.

A few hours later, Jack heard through another employee that his direct report had cleaned out his office and left a letter of resignation on his desk, stating that he was ashamed of the error he had made and could no longer work in a place where the "cloud of shame" hung over him. With hindsight, Jack realized that his direct report's silence had been a bit odd, that it had been strained and tense. At the time, though, he had been more intent on delivering his message than on interpreting his direct report's reaction.

- Bowed head

In Asian and Middle Eastern cultures, a bowed head is often a symbol of submission. In Hindu cultures, it's a sign of deep respect. Typically, bowing one's body is deferential and often linked to a country's religion—for example, Muslims bow in prayer, as do followers of other religions.

If your direct report bows his head as you speak to him—especially if you're in a room with other people—something may be wrong. It may be that you've shamed him in some way you're not aware of, and his body language is communicating to you that he has lost face. Pay attention to whether other people have their heads bowed. If not, you need to address this issue in some way so you can save face for your employee.

- Hasty exit

In the West, there's the expression, "I was so embarrassed, I wished I could disappear." In developing countries, a loss of face evokes similar feelings. Your people may act on that feeling by suddenly departing from a meeting or any group function. They may offer an excuse of not feeling well or having another appointment, but it may be a sign that they feel they've lost respect and can't stand to be in the presence of others—the others are bearing witness to the shame, and this is intolerable.

- Absence

Someone may call in sick or take a vacation day or not show up for an event that you assumed he would attend. While everyone gets sick or takes a day off now and then, this behavior can also be a sign that someone has lost face. Watch for repeated patterns of absence—when people don't show up more than once for a given event or when there is something unusual or causative about an absence (for example, your direct report didn't receive a promotion and then failed to show up for a meeting the next day).

A New Approach to Delegating

In the West, managers are encouraged to become expert delegators. Managers who are too controlling not only hamper the development of their own people but become enmeshed in carrying out tasks and fail to devote sufficient time to higher-level thinking and planning. In a developing country, however, managers have to be wary of delegating too much too soon for two reasons related to saving face.

First, as the equivalent of the village elder, you'll find that employees will accept decisions you make more readily than those made by your direct reports. You may declare that you've decided not to invite certain employees to attend a trade show, and if you handle it in the right way (appeasing them using other recognition tools, for instance), they won't lose face. If your direct report makes this decision, however, this may have a different impact on employees because he lacks the status of village elder. They may find his decision demeaning and feel they've lost face because of it.

Second, when you delegate decision-making authority, your direct reports may lack savvy about face issues, especially if they're from the West (though we've seen managers who are native to developing countries who have their own personal reasons for causing others to lose face).

For this reason, you need to delegate decision-making authority more gradually than you might in the West, and when you do delegate it, you need to provide your people with air cover. In other words, own decisions jointly with them so you provide your mantle of authority for the choices they make. Consult with them prior to the decision and talk about the face issues involved and how to manage them. In this way, you'll ease them into their new roles with a higher level of awareness regarding saving face.

Putting Face in Perspective

Finally, as you've been reading this chapter, you may still say to yourself that you're a manager who is direct, focused on results, and holds people accountable, that you won't change this style in order to placate overly sensitive employees. One manager, who found himself struggling with his people's face issues when he worked in an Asian country, said, "I understand that people don't like to be told they made a mistake when other people are around, but they need to get over it. Sometimes there just isn't time to have private, one-on-one talks, and sometimes feeling bad about what you did is motivation for learning and growth."

We might add that you—like this manager—may be convinced that at least some people will get past the face issue and learn to function like Western employees. Perhaps you've worked with individuals in developing countries who have developed thick skins and who are more concerned with growing as professionals than with saving face.

No doubt, some people do transcend their cultures and learn to work with the same mind-set as those raised in the United States and Europe. But some don't, and that's a problem. If half your people feel they have lost face, you'll experience a huge decline in morale and productivity. Consequently, it makes sense to take these face issues seriously.

Understand the difference between what sociologists refer to as a collective society versus an individualistic society. If you're like most people who have grown up in the West, you were raised in cultures where individuals are on their own—you are measured by what you accomplish, and you are rewarded for your results. Grades, hiring criteria, political success—all are focused on individual accomplishment.

In collective societies, on the other hand, families, communities, religious groups, royal families, and political parties are all seen as more important than the individual. For these groups to function effectively, written and unwritten rules focus on avoiding conflict. Everyone has a place within the hierarchies of these groups, and the social norms in these countries help people maintain this place. The group leader generally is skilled at helping people maintain their social standing and at avoiding conflicts, hurt feelings, and win–loss scenarios that are common in individualistic societies.

Consider, too, that these collective societies have existed for thousands of years and their cultures are deeply embedded. Do not be so quick to think that you can change the impact of these cultures on employees overnight—or over a period of weeks or months. Saving face is a reality in many developing countries, and a wise manager will recognize this reality and work with it or around it.

CHAPTER 7

Manage Flexibly in Ambiguous, Volatile Environments

You may have worked in an industry that has gone through roller-coaster cycles or for a company that has been restructured, but these situations are different from the volatile, unpredictable environment you are going to encounter in a developing country. To a certain extent, change in the West is controlled and expected. Even if it feels chaotic as a company restructures or is acquired, in the United States or Europe these events take place within a familiar framework. While you may be upset by the changes that are going on around you, you generally understand the logic of the moves being made and the consequences for you and others.

In many developing countries, however, change often comes out of the blue. One day everything is running smoothly, but the next day the factory is shut down by governmental decree. One day you have the funding for a project, and the next day you don't. One day you have a direct report who you've groomed to take on major responsibilities, and the next day you hear that he's needed by his family to help out during a crisis in a remote province and won't be back for at least a month.

While the degree and frequency of change varies from one country to the next, as a rule, you should expect that degree and frequency to be much higher than in the West. If you're a manager who is a my-way-or-the-highway type of person, then you're going to struggle in this environment. If you adhere to one approach or have trouble shifting your plans on the fly, then you're going to be frustrated.

We've found that adaptability is a critical trait for managers and leaders in developing nations. We're using this term in the broadest possible sense. It means being flexible when your best-laid plans go awry; it means being tolerant of ambiguity, confusion, and uncertainty, and it means being able to react quickly and creatively when events mandate new strategies and tactics.

Before focusing on how to put a flexible mindset into practice, though, let's look at the various common occurrences that make this mindset essential.

Every Day Holds a Surprise

When Bob was working in Dubai, one of DAE's primary goals was to expand its airport management division worldwide—helping other countries create more efficient, effective airports. This effort was encouraged by Dubai's government, which believed that this would foster better relationships with Western powers. At first things went well, and it seemed as if this would be a profitable endeavor. Then, inexplicably, the government's policy shifted. All of a sudden, the government no longer provided encouragement and support for the airport strategy.

No one communicated that support was being withdrawn. No one told Bob that he should scale back his efforts in this area. At first, he and other executives were bewildered. They had been told this was a priority, and now it wasn't. The company had invested a great deal of money and time in its airport group, and its efforts to date had been profitable. What was Bob supposed to do?

What he did was try to learn the reasons for the change in governmental policy. Though it wasn't easy to discover the truth, he eventually found out that some bureaucrats in these Western countries viewed DAE's strategy as threatening on a number of fronts. They feared that DAE would take away jobs from citizens of their countries, and they felt that DAE, and Dubai by extension, was an interloper, attempting to take over functions that these countries felt should remain in their hands. When Dubai government officials felt this resistance to DAE's efforts, they withdrew support. To save face, however, they didn't communicate what they were doing because it would have been an admission of shortsightedness.

Bob could have responded in a number of ways. He could have confronted government officials and demanded the full support they had promised initially. He could have persisted in the strategy with the hope that because it was profitable, it would eventually regain support. Instead, he adapted the strategy to the situation.

When Bob understood what had happened, he had his airport group target other developing countries, such as India, that were eager for help in creating better airports. Though this was not as profitable an approach as the previous one, it allowed DAE to continue to derive value from its resources in this sector.

We have found that surprises like this one are the rule rather than the exception in every developing country we've worked in; there are times when things happen that make no sense, at least to the Western mind. To adapt effectively, it helps to be aware of the most common categories of surprises:

- Governmental interventions

This can take many forms, including the one just mentioned in the previous story where the government shifts its policy covertly and forces a company to operate differently. But we've experienced and heard stories about other governmental moves that have created confusion among corporate leaders and managers. For instance, a government may pass a new law or enact a new policy to extort money or other favors from a company—the policy is rescinded when the company does what is requested. Sometimes, of course, it is impossible to figure out what a government wants in return for rescinding the law or policy—no government official wants to be direct about being an extortionist. We've also talked to leaders who tell us of being caught in complex political intrigues—one political faction wants to gain power by aligning itself with the company's leaders while another faction hopes to cater to the populist element by taking a stand against the company. And there are instances when government bureaucrats will suddenly make demands of a corporation—partner with us on building a water reservoir, provide us with a 300-page report of all the transactions you've conducted in the past year—that seem arbitrary yet can be enormously time-consuming and costly.

- Economic changes

In the West, budgets tend to be sacred objects. People adhere to them with religious fervor, knowing that they will be held accountable for staying within budget. In developing countries, budgets are often seen as nothing more than guidelines and are not taken as seriously. It may seem as if there's no money in the budget for a project, yet if the company leaders or powerful groups in the country want the project undertaken, the money magically appears. Conversely, it may seem as if financial resources exist to launch a new project or product, but suddenly you're informed that the money isn't there.

Bob recalls that in Dubai he operated on the assumption that the company's investors would provide him with the money needed to implement the strategies they had discussed and approved. Yet, this was a Western assumption. He began to realize that his assumption was erroneous when money for projects flowed much more slowly than he had expected. Then the money stopped at the same time as Dubai experienced an economic downturn—there was no separation of state and private industry as there is in the West. Bob responded by trying a number of approaches: he suggested finding other investors; he asked the sheikh to intervene with current investors and get them to loosen the purse strings, and he created what he referred to as "early tragedy dates"—setting deadlines for funding projects one month earlier than the real due dates, providing a one-month cushion in which to find the money that had not yet arrived.

Infrastructure in developing countries is much more fragile than in the West, and damage or shifts in infrastructure affect just about every organization that operates within these countries' borders. Natural disasters like hurricanes, earthquakes, fires, floods, and the like can impact a private company's financial resources—subsidies or partnering funds the company is receiving from the government can dry up instantly. Civil unrest and regime change can have similar effects. And in countries where dictators rule, the person at the top can have a change of heart or shift his priorities and arbitrarily abrogate done deals.

- Moving time frames

Again, people in the West tend to take deadlines and timelines more seriously than people in developing countries do. They are not in as much of a rush to get things done, and as a number of executives we interviewed remarked, this has to do with their very different philosophy of time: they are not burdened with the same short-term thinking and impatience that many Western leaders possess. Rather, they believe that things get done in their own time and that delays serve a larger purpose that may not be discerned at the time they occur.

In addition, getting things done on time in developing countries is often more problematic for practical reasons. Sometimes companies discover that the supplier they were going to rely on for a product launch cannot provide them with the needed quantity of materials on a timely basis, or they learn that vested interests outside the company—government officials, religious leaders, union heads—would prefer that a project go forward more slowly—or more quickly.

For example, Henry took a job as the senior vice president of a midsized manufacturing company in China. One of Henry's main responsibilities was acquisitions—the company was highly profitable and eager to expand. Henry knew of a company in a Western country that he thought highly of and that he felt would be a perfect acquisition candidate. He did his due diligence, and after getting the green light from his CEO he made an offer to the company that was accepted. The deadline for the acquisition was rapidly approaching when Henry's CEO called him into his office and said they had a problem: a local government official who was well connected to the central government in Beijing had gotten wind of the acquisition and was holding it up. He was telling the CEO that it would take him at least a few months until he had reviewed and filled out all the necessary paperwork. Henry asked the CEO if the official was looking for a bribe, but the CEO said that wasn't it. Apparently, this official had had a bad experience with the Western country where the acquisition target was located and was slowing down the acquisition process out of spite.

Henry came close to quitting. As much as he liked the job, this wasn't the first time that he felt frustrated by a situation he couldn't understand. Fortunately, though, Henry had been there long enough to understand that if one approach didn't work, it was important to try a second or third one. At first, he tried to convince the CEO to use his influence with certain government officials to overrule the local party official who was creating a roadblock to the acquisition. The CEO protested that he didn't want to risk offending the local official, whose brother was a senior member of the government's Central Committee. Then Henry tried to argue that the financial cost of losing the deal would be significant—that there were penalties built in to the acquisition agreement that the Chinese company would incur if it didn't complete the acquisition by the date in the agreement. The CEO shrugged and said that it would just have to be this way.

Then Henry noted that the media in this Western country had covered the acquisition negotiations extensively and that if the Chinese company failed to acquire the company by the given date, there would be a great deal of negative publicity. The CEO seemed very concerned by this possibility and managed to overcome the opposition of the local official and allow the company to complete the acquisition by the deadline. With hindsight, Henry suspected that the possible loss of face motivated the CEO to take action.

- Individual employee reactions.

This is probably the area that holds the most surprises. Because of cultural differences, Western managers and native employees don't always share the same work habits and sensibilities. More than one of the executives we interviewed talked about inadvertently offending a direct report. These Western leaders often had no idea that they had done something that employees found disrespectful. A number of them shared stories about employees whose behavior was bewildering. One refused to work on a project and would not explain his refusal. Another requested a transfer because he was letting his boss down even though his boss insisted he didn't feel this way. A third began arriving at the office at the crack of dawn and leaving hours after everyone else had left. When his Western manager asked why he was putting in so many more hours than other employees, this employee replied that he believed the company was in trouble (it wasn't) and that he thought he should do his part of help out. A fourth insisted that he be given special privileges because he was of a higher caste than his fellow employees—privileges that included a longer lunch break and an office that he didn't have to share with colleagues.

When Rob was in Dubai helping DAE plan an important meeting, he met with a DAE marketing executive to talk about the requirements for the room where the meeting was to be held. When Rob arrived at the hotel and inspected the room prior to the meeting, he found that things had not been arranged according to the specifications agreed upon. He contacted this marketing executive, a Dubai citizen, and requested that some changes be made to the room. Rob emphasized that he was extremely respectful in his request, and he didn't think about it again—until he learned that the marketing executive never returned to work. For a reason that remains unclear to this day, this executive responded to Rob's request by leaving the company suddenly and without explanation.

- Work schedules and environments

This may seem like a small thing relative to the other four issues we just discussed, but we can guarantee that you're going to be surprised by some employees' reactions when you request they work overtime, assign them a new office, or insist they participate on a particular team.

Earlier we talked about two individuals who were involved in a blood feud and had such antipathy for each other that each plotted the other's downfall. When you observed them, however, they spoke politely to each other, never betraying their animosity in public. But it was impossible for them to work together productively. Whether the animosity is tribal, religious, or personal, you're going to encounter employees who simply cannot work together. The problem is that most Western managers don't recognize this fact until it's too late—and productivity has been lost.

Similarly, some people will refuse to work certain days of the week or certain hours of the day. There are religious or cultural holidays that you might know nothing about. In parts of Asia, Friday is prayer day, and if employees do work, they will expect to have time off during the day for prayers. While people in some cultures will want and expect overtime, others will view any time outside of the stated working days and hours as their own time and resent any violation of this work principle.

Also, saving face can play a huge role in how people react to decisions or other actions that may strike you as minor. A change in title or office space can evoke major negative or positive reactions. Choosing one person for a team and not another can be interpreted by the chosen one as equivalent to a promotion and by the one not chosen as a message that he should quit.

Developing a Flexible Style

Given all the inexplicable behaviors and sudden changes we just described, a rigid or doctrinaire approach tends to be untenable in developing countries. In the West, executives are usually consistent in their management style. They like to tell their people that "this is how I am; you know what you can expect of me," or words to that effect. In short, they expect their people to adapt to them.

In developing countries, it's far more effective when executives adapt to others. Adaptability, however, isn't something that comes naturally to many Western leaders. As one manager who worked in both China and Russia put it, "You need to slow down your managerial reaction time so you can be more thoughtful in how you deal with different people and situations."

The following three suggestions will help you slow down and become more flexible in your management style:

• Be a sponge.

In other words, absorb as much information as possible before reacting or making a decision. Get to know your people; figure out the two individuals in your group who may not be able to work well together under any circumstances; become attuned to the political climate and labor strikes or other types of civil unrest on the horizon; figure out who tends to get things done in your company and why and how (and what doesn't work); learn who the difficult customers and suppliers are and the best ways to deal with them; and listen when people talk about how various government agencies or other powerful entities (religious groups, political factions, etc.) in the country impact how the company functions.

It may take a few weeks or a few months to absorb sufficient knowledge, but at that point, you can design an approach that is situational. You need to be pragmatic rather than dogmatic, able to adjust everything from your relationships with direct reports to your decision-making process on major projects. The more you absorb about your organization, its people, and the relevant external variables, the easier it will be to adapt to what's happening in the company and the country.

- Rely on forethought.

It stands to reason that Western managers aren't going to understand at least some of their employees in a developing country and that they're not going to understand them as well as they do people who grew up in cultures and companies similar to their own. For example, Allison was a young consultant for a firm based in the United States and had been working in Bangalore, helping professionalize an Indian company's inbound telemarketing efforts. One of the people she was working with, Kumar, was a forty-something manager of ten inbound operators, and he struck Allison as smart and well-educated. Yet, there were times when she requested he make a change in how his people dealt with callers, and he seemed to ignore her request. This didn't happen all the time but usually about every third request. When she confronted him about this issue, he would just make excuses, and she suspected he wasn't leveling with her.

It was only after talking to a colleague of Kumar's that she got the truth. It turned out that Kumar was raised in a village where cultural dictated that younger women never speak harshly to older men—it was considered a sign of disrespect. Though Allison didn't think she ever spoke harshly to him, she knew that if she was under pressure or frustrated, a hard edge crept into her tone. After gaining this knowledge, Allison was highly conscious of how she interacted with Kumar, making it a point to calm herself down and speak evenly with him. And from then on, he was much more accommodating of her requests.

Admittedly, forethought can be a time-consuming pain. You don't have to use it for every single interaction and decision, but it should be relied on more than in the West, especially when you're dealing with difficult people or making important decisions involving hiring, firing, performance reviews, and so on. If it helps, consider what professional basketball coach Phil Jackson wrote about the value of forethought in his book, *Sacred Hoops* (1995); he explained that when he was coaching the Chicago Bulls, he had both Michael Jordan and Dennis Rodman on his team, two very different people with different motivations. As a result, he created a process for dealing with each of them that involved a great deal of forethought. He figured out a tailored approach that would drive each player to reach his potential, and his flexibility was crucial for getting the most from each and helping the Bulls win championships.

- Go with the flow.

Managers in the West place a lot of faith in time frames, planning, and objectives. They "fix" all of this in ink on paper (or figurative ink on computer screens), and this plan provides direction for what a large number of people do every day at work. Yet, because of all the sudden changes in developing countries and the difficulty of understanding people, this fixed mind-set can often be more destructive than productive. Instead of providing guidance for completion of a program or project, it becomes a straitjacket that inhibits necessary on-the-fly changes.

Going with the flow, therefore, means refusing to lock yourself into a specific timetable or plan. It's great to have these tools, but be willing to adjust them as circumstances change. There will be delays. You might have to scale down your goals. You may need to shuffle the members of your team in midstream to complete a project. Western managers are often loath to make these adjustments, since in the West doing so suggests that they were shortsighted in their planning or have lost control of a project or the people working on it. In a developing country, however, a go-with-the-flow mind-set not only provides the flexibility to adapt to unexpected situations, but it gives Western managers a perspective that helps them accept the confusion and volatility they encounter.

Tactical Responses: What Should I Do When...

"Expect the unexpected" should be the mantra of every Western manager working in a developing country. The previous suggestions in terms of developing a flexible style will help guide you through the surprises you encounter, but more specific, situation-based advice is also necessary. To that end, here are some common surprises you're likely to encounter and some tips on how to handle them flexibly and effectively:

- What should I do when something goes wrong suddenly and I have to deliver bad or negative news?

It can be anything from the failure of a system to your people failing to handle an assignment effectively. Murphy's Law holds that if something can go wrong, it will go wrong, and this is especially true when you're working in a place with a volatile political system, a fragile economy, employees who may have their jobs more because of who they know rather than what they know, and equipment or technology that may be old and subject to breakdowns. Because of this environment, things can go wrong fast. It may be a minor mistake of a direct report or a major collapse of a system, but whatever it is, you have to address it.

Most Western managers lose some degree of control in response to bad news and screwups. Some scream and curse. Others tend to be critical of the individuals who made the mistake or deliver diatribes about the incompetence of a system, process, or group of people.

In a developing country, you'll be better served if you recall our "sponge" advice in the previous section and absorb the blow, keeping your emotions in check as you take in information and then communicate with your people. If you shame and blame others, you're just going to make a bad situation worse. Not only do people in developing countries tend to think poorly of leaders who lose control in public situations, but they are acutely sensitive to blame and shame because of the face issues we discussed in the preceding chapter.

Focus on delivering the facts. By relying on data to respond to bad news, you give yourself a variety of options.

If a system breaks down, talk about the data that reveals the breakdown. If someone let you down, communicate the specific, factual consequences of this behavior. You can capture the data and communicate it in writing as well as verbally. You can go into a lot of detail about what the facts signify or you can deliver broad-brush interpretations. You may find that there's a lot of data to discuss, so you can divide your delivery of it into a series of meetings.

We've found that people in developing nations are no strangers to bad news—many of your employees will have had to deal with everything from floods to disease to wars to famines. In many ways, they're more adept at rebounding from it than employees in the West. But they need leaders who can interpret the situations factually and give them the information necessary for them to formulate an effective response. They don't need or want leaders who blow up emotionally—this one-note response to bad news will turn off your people.

- What should do if I'm faced with a situation where people are responding in ways that seem ambiguous or strange?

This happens all the time. For example, one manager who worked in China said he had an employee who "never cracked a smile or frowned; he just looked at me with a blank stare, and it wasn't because he didn't understand English because he did." We've heard other complaints from executives in different countries about people who didn't take work seriously, and about individuals who took it too seriously. And a manager who worked for a European company in Africa told us about a direct report who seemed like a different person every day—one day he'd dress and act just like an employee in the West, and the next he'd wear strange outfits and be belligerent and uncooperative.

But the most common complaints we've heard—and the most vexing—are employees managers can't read. Western executives can't tell if their people are happy or sad, angry or satisfied, interested or disinterested. We've worked with people who seem to grasp assignments in conversations about what they're supposed to do, yet they can't implement them effectively. We have hammered out agreements during a meeting, but afterward it was as if the agreements were figments of our imaginations and the issues were still up for discussion. It's frustrating to have employees you can't figure out, and a common reaction is to write them off—to assume they're playing games with you or are just damaged individuals who are unable to respond appropriately to work assignments.

In fact, ambiguity is a common response in cultures where a foreigner from the West is in charge. Employees feel they need to play their cards close to the vest. They think that if they allow the boss (whom they don't understand either) to see who they really are, they are making themselves vulnerable and that the boss might not like who they are and get rid of them. The cause of ambiguity may be the emotional maturity issue we discussed earlier. In a business setting, especially, some people's maturity is low, and they don't know the appropriate way to respond to a Western boss, and so they choose the "safer" neutral demeanor. And their ambiguous mien may stem from other issues—fear (for example, they had a cruel boss before and found ambiguity was the best way to deal with him) or resentment (for example, they believe that a native of their country should be their boss).

Because ambiguity has different causes, you need to be flexible in dealing with it. There's an expression that's useful in this regard: "Stay longer and deeper in the process." What this means is that you have to wait longer and dig deeper before responding to ambiguity. Time and your own investigative powers should help you better understand what your direct report's hard-to-read reactions signify. Creating feedback loops is a great idea—you want to give your people regular opportunities to talk to you about assignments, problems, and so on. In this way, you'll learn enough to read an ambiguous reaction and know what it signifies. With that knowledge, you'll find it much easier to respond effectively.

- What should I do when I'm blindsided by a major change that throws a wrench into my plans?

What you should not do is overreact. One of the people we interviewed told us that he was hired by a South American company that had just had its best fiscal year in its thirty-year history, and two months after this executive was hired, it fired 20 percent of its staff (this executive was hired expressly for his skill in crafting growth strategies). As we've mentioned, volatility is a fact of life. If you panic and people see you lose control, then you'll never regain your managerial standing in their eyes.

Here's a sampling of the major plan-altering changes you might experience while working in a developing country:

- Major, unexpected cuts are made to your budget.
- The government suddenly informs you of a new regulation that forces you to change the way you do business.

- Your workers go out on strike.
- Rolling blackouts are instituted because of mismanagement of the utility company.
- The threat of terrorism requires you to institute new security procedures.
- Regime change creates conditions that are less favorable (or, in some instances, more favorable) to your business strategy.

While you should heed our earlier management style advice in these situations—go with the flow—a more proactive piece of advice is to find "forecasters" to help you anticipate surprises. Invariably, there are people in your workplace who had an inkling of the event that took you by surprise. Typically, they're the "old salts" of the company or individuals with governmental, religious, and tribal or royal affiliations. Get to know them. Build trust with them. Rely on them and reward them for forecasts. If you know in advance what business-changing events are in the offing, you'll be better able to adjust your plans accordingly.

Know Your Type and Break It

In the West, most managers develop a style that works for them. Some are decisive hard-charging leaders; others become known as people persons; still others are seen as great implementers, and there are those who are viewed as idea people. There are many other styles, and they often are effective, but in developing countries a single style limits your flexibility. Even worse, when you're under stress (as you will be in many positions in a developing country), you revert to the style that you know best and that has worked for you in the past. You become even more rigid in your approach, and this can be counterproductive in an environment where there's a surprise around every corner.

Therefore, make a conscious effort to vary your style. For example:

- If you usually make decisions based on the data, give yourself license to rely on your instincts in certain situations.
- If you are more a doer than a thinker, force yourself to spend some time reflecting on issues before taking action.
- If you tend to have quick, to-the-point discussions with your people, make an effort to have longer, more wide-ranging talks.

The point is to test a variety of approaches to management issues so that you're not locked into a single approach. This doesn't guarantee that you'll be flexible every time you face a rapidly changing situation, but it increases your capacity for flexibility, and that capacity can serve you well in a country where every day brings a fresh surprise.

A Crucial Leadership Competency

Finally, we would be remiss if we didn't point out that this particular principle is becoming as important in the West as it is in developing countries. In fact, any organization in the West that wants to increase the capacity of its leaders to adapt to rapidly changing circumstances should send them on a six-month tour of duty in a developing country.

One executive who worked in India told us his mantra was, "Adapt or die." Working in India, China, Costa Rica, or just about any country with chaotic, rapidly evolving environments helps make leaders become more flexible in a variety of ways.

Perhaps most important, it provides them with firsthand evidence that the style or method they have relied on for years and that has proved to be effective isn't the only style or method that works. Leaders and managers may grasp this point cognitively, but it's usually only when they have real-life evidence that they change their behavior accordingly.

Second, their tenure in developing countries gives them the chance to test new ideas, fresh tactics, and unfamiliar styles of managing. The odds are they would not test any of these new ways of doing business unless they were forced by necessity to try them—the pressures to be flexible remain greater in developing countries than in the West. In fact, some of the leaders we talked to said they tried a new approach not because they wanted to but because they had no other choice—their traditional way of doing things wasn't effective.

Third, they are faced with numerous situations that require flexibility. Just about every day demands that they try something new and different. One day they have to implement a new policy for hiring—one they would have never tried in the United States. The next day, they must figure out how to motivate a direct report who is talented but unresponsive to all the conventional motivational tactics. The sheer number of instances where executives are required to be flexible, then, has a much more powerful effect than if they only needed be flexible a few times each year.

Even if this is your last assignment in a developing country, it can provide dividends for your jobs in the United States and Europe for years to come. While the environment in these Western nations may never be as volatile or chaotic as in developing states, it seems inevitable that it will become increasingly unpredictable and confusing. Given this inevitability, leaders who can adapt and adjust will be increasingly valuable to all types of organizations.

CHAPTER 8

Get Out of Limbo

Limbo is an unfamiliar business concept to most Western executives, so the best way we can introduce it is by telling you a story about it.

Josh worked for a large Chinese consumer products corporation in Shanghai and ran their small but growing new products division. Josh had been with the company and in China for almost a year, and after getting acclimated to the job during the first few months, his focus had been on a new product launch for a line of toys. Everyone at the company, from the CEO to many of his senior vice presidents, had told Josh that they were excited about the launch and that he would receive whatever financial support and other resources he needed to help make the launch successful. Josh found that they backed up those words with actions. When an equipment glitch occurred in the plant that was supposed to manufacture the toys, the vice president of manufacturing stepped in and helped remedy the situation as soon as Josh informed him of the problem.

Josh was therefore befuddled when the date of the launch was fast approaching and he received an email from his boss that the launch needed to be delayed by a month or so. Josh was concerned since he felt all elements of the launch—the publicity campaign, the distribution arrangement, and so on—had to be synchronized for maximum effectiveness. A conversation with his boss, though, reassured Josh. His boss explained to Josh that there were factors beyond his control that he couldn't discuss at the moment that had forced him to delay the introduction. "But don't worry," he said to Josh. "I'm sure we'll give you the green light soon."

But the green light was not forthcoming. Josh again talked to his boss about the delay and was again reassured that approval was imminent. But it did not come. Josh talked to other senior executives, and they were as maddeningly vague as his own boss. Each supplied a credible though rather weak reason for the delay. One said that the issue was a competitor's launch of a similar product line at the same time. Another explained that there was a minor financial roadblock because the company had incurred an unexpected cost at the end of the quarter. At first they all agreed with his boss and said approval would come soon. Then, they told him to be patient and that the launch might have to wait until later in the year. Then Josh's boss told him he really wasn't sure when he might be given the go-ahead but that the launch was definitely "not dead."

In this case, however, it was dead for the foreseeable future, but no one would acknowledge this fact. It was still listed as an active project in all the company's correspondence and planning reports. People still talked to Josh about the launch as if it were going to happen relatively soon. But in reality, the project was in limbo.

Josh never discovered the real reason why his new product line was put on the back burner, and though he was with the company for another five years, it was never taken off the back burner. But this indirect, indefinite postponement of projects and programs is not uncommon in developing nations. This is what we mean by limbo, and if you find yourself in it, you need to find a way out of it.

What Limbo Is Like

In the West, when management puts the kibosh on your project, you know about it right away. Bosses don't care if they promised you that you could pursue a task or try out a new concept. If they have a change of heart, they will let you know about it. They're not shy about telling you that they no longer have the funding or that they need you to work on something else or that strategic rethinking mandates other priorities.

Similarly, if a project really still is a go but has been delayed, your bosses will generally be straight with you on this matter as well. Your boss will tell you that your group has overspent for the year and so your initiative will have to wait until the next fiscal year. You'll be given a time frame for reviving your project or team and a realistic projection of when you can get back to work on it. Sometimes, of course, one delay begets another, and it's possible that a delay will turn into a stop. But when management decides to end something they previously okayed, they'll be straightforward about it, no matter how embarrassed they are (though often they are not embarrassed at all).

In many developing countries, however, management takes a very different approach to these situations. Sometimes, management's reluctance to be straightforward about these issues and proclaim a promised project dead has to do with saving face. Managers don't want to make a public admission that they said one thing and are now doing another; they don't want to have a confrontation with you in which you remind them of this failure or you complain to others about it. Limbo, then, is a face-saving alternative.

Sometimes, though, the reasons behind limbo are more complex. For instance, your boss may not want to admit the real reason why your initiative has been stopped. It may be that the CEO arbitrarily decided he didn't like your strategy. It may be that what you planned to do clashed with the agenda of some powerful individual inside or outside the company. It may be that someone protested that you were too young, too junior, or too foreign to be allowed to pursue a project before someone else. It may be that you unknowingly offended someone who responded by pulling some strings and getting your strategy discarded. It may be that the company realized it didn't know how to execute the plan you proposed or that it lacked the expertise necessary to implement it.

It's also possible that it's not just one of these reasons but two or more of them, inextricably woven together. They form a barrier to implementation, and it's possible that no one ever had a formal meeting and declared your project dead or pushed to the back burner, but they simply saw the

barrier, acknowledged it, and stopped providing funding
or other resources that would allow you to move forward.
Unlike companies in the West, your organization may
operate without a structured approval process, and senior
managers may make decisions on some matters (usually for
face-saving purposes) privately and indirectly.

But limbo can be even more complicated than what we've
just described. Remember, limbo doesn't always mean that
a project is kaput. In many developing countries, patience
truly is a virtue. Companies there are not as obsessed as
Western companies with rigid scorecards and time frames.
They like sitting with a concept or strategy for a while, letting it gather support or opposition over time. They reason,
not incorrectly, that if they give it time, the strengths and
weaknesses of an approach will emerge and help the company reach a more effective decision.

A distaste for being measured also contributes to limbo.
Many people in developing countries, especially those in the
managerial ranks, are accustomed to working in ambiguous
environments. If they don't give the go-ahead to projects
that carry some risk, they won't be held accountable if they
fail. They often prefer the safe, low-reward strategy to the
risky, high-reward one. They may make a show of verbally
applauding your great idea and indicate that they would love
to see you get it off the ground, but they can't pull the trigger.
They may want to pull it—they recognize the idea's value,
and they get caught up in the excitement surrounding the
idea—but when they recognize that green-lighting the idea
exposes them to censure or worse, they get cold feet.

Recognize, too, that limbo often occurs when you're
trying to get something done that entails a degree of risk

or creativity and requires an investment of time, money, or other resources. You're pushing to obtain approval from at least the managerial layer above you and possibly from layers above that. Typically, the first response from your bosses is approval, assuming your concept is viable. They applaud your ingenuity, your daring, and your focus on long-term growth and profit. You feel certain that formal approval for your plan or idea is just around the corner. Then nothing happens, and you make inquiries and receive positive responses. It sounds as if the reasons for the delay are reasonable and should soon vanish. The longer you wait, though, the more you wonder whether anything is going to happen. Unbeknownst to you, your boss has moved your idea up a layer, and his boss may have moved the idea up yet another layer, but somewhere along the line, resistance to the idea forms. Your boss doesn't want to admit that he couldn't convince his boss to give him the go-ahead for your idea, or his boss doesn't want to admit that he couldn't make a strong enough case to his boss. Again, saving face is the factor that prevents people from being open and honest with you about what is really happening. Eventually, someone might suggest that you move on to other projects for the moment, but they still will not admit that your project is dead.

Signs of Limbo

We are making limbo sound easier to identify than it actually is. As one executive working in a developing country told us, "I was naively optimistic. Everyone was telling me my program was still viable, and so despite all the excuses

and delays I believed it." As a general rule, Western business people are naively optimistic. Relentlessly logical and
results-oriented, they assume that if someone doesn't put
forth a good reason for a project going forward, it eventually
will go forward since it's in the company's best interest for
this to happen.

Succumbing to this naive optimism, however, can turn
your job in a developing country into an extremely frustrating
one. More than that, it can prevent you from accomplishing
tasks that are crucial for your career and your company. You
need to find a way out of limbo, and the first step is recognizing that what you're in is really limbo rather than a temporary
delay.

Heed these five signs of limbo:

1. Big gap between approval and action. This gap often
   signifies that no action is forthcoming. While there's
   often a small gap between receiving the go-ahead and
   actual implementation, when the interval stretches out
   for weeks or months, the delay indicates a problem.
   Generally, you know what an appropriate gap is between
   approval and action for a given project (though, obviously, the length of this gap can vary, and it's usually
   longer if there's more risk or money involved). When a
   one-month gap becomes a three-month delay, then you
   know that something is wrong.
2. Lack of a straight answer. For example, Steve was working for a US-based division of a company in Southeast
   Asia, but his boss as well as most of the senior managers were from this Southeast Asian country. Steve, a
   technology expert, had suggested major technological

changes in all the company's plants in that country. His boss had praised his ideas but said he needed approval from the country head and the company chief financial officer before they could proceed. Shortly thereafter, Steve's boss reported that he had received "tentative approval," but that they wanted to study his recommendations in more detail before they allowed him to proceed. When nothing happened, Steve asked his boss for the cause of the delay. At first, his boss told him that his plan was still under study. A few weeks later when Steve asked again, his boss said that they had completed their study but explained that now they wanted to survey the heads of their various plants to get their input. A few weeks after that, Steve's boss told him that the plant heads were in favor of Steve's recommendations, but they wanted to wait until the next fiscal year before implementing them. Thus, Steve should have recognized that not only wasn't he getting a straight answer, but the answers kept changing—another sign of limbo.

3. The idea/project becomes an "undiscussable." People change the subject when you start asking questions (this may happen after they've given you a number of vague or contradictory answers for why things aren't moving forward). Sometimes deftly, sometimes awkwardly, they avoid answering your question about what's holding up implementation. When something is in limbo, people assume you'll take the hint and drop the subject—they figure that you'll understand nothing is happening and won't be so gauche as to ask a question to which you already know the answer. But as a Western business person, you expect a direct yes or no. Rather than give

it to you, your boss and other executives steer clear of the topic you want to address.

4. Illogical "I don't know" answers. You hear this from your boss, your boss's boss, and colleagues. Obviously, you hear the same articulations of lack of knowledge in the West, but our modifier "illogical" suggests that the people concerned should know even though they claim they don't. Claiming ignorance is a common fallback position in developing countries, and it's also a sign of limbo.

5. Outright lies. This often happens when you refuse to allow the topic to be an undiscussable or to accept the "I don't know" answers. The more you push for a direct answer, the more likely you'll invite a lie. For example, Maria, a senior executive for a company in Ecuador, had been asked by her boss to lead a team that was going to restructure the organization. Maria worked tirelessly for months on the restructuring plan with her team, and when they submitted it, the plan won universal praise and approval from the management team. Yet nothing happened for weeks, and despite Maria's repeated requests for updates on where the plan stood, she received mostly vague answers from her boss and others. Finally, Maria and two members of her team confronted their boss and demanded to know why their approved restructuring plan wasn't being implemented. He explained that the main problem was that their plan called for the elimination of a number of middle-management jobs, and one of the jobs targeted was held by a man whose father was one of the richest men in the country. This employee somehow had gotten wind of

the restructuring plan, complained to his father, and the latter had intervened with the company's CEO and had him scrap the restructuring. This sounded credible to Maria and her colleagues until she spoke to someone who knew this middle manager well, and Maria learned that his father was a relatively poor farmer. Maria never learned why the restructuring had been put on indefinite hold, but she learned that a lie was a sign of limbo.

Finally, be aware that sometimes limbo is indicated by cognitive dissonance—you know what should be happening, but something else is taking place instead. If you're a veteran leader or manager, you have a good sense of how a project should be implemented or of the time frame for a new program or policy to be rolled out. You are keenly aware of the steps that lead from conception to execution. Thus, you know when a clash is occurring between your expectations and reality.

In Dubai, one of DAE's strategies was to create an aerospace engineering/pilot training university. This would not only provide needed employees for the company but would provide employment and future career opportunities for many of Dubai's citizens. Bob helped found this university, and things went well during the first two years. During planning and budgeting for the next two years when the university staff and classes were set to be expanded, Bob and his people encountered subtle resistance from the company's investors. When they submitted the estimated costs for years three and four, the investors stalled. The final decision on the budget started bouncing around between three groups— the investors, the government, and the country's airline.

No one said no. In fact, it seemed as if they needed more information about the success of the university during the first two years—it had achieved its objectives—so Bob and his team assembled the data and presented it. They were certain they were making a convincing case for the investors to fund the next two years, but instead the investors started talking about how they were "business people, not educators" and wanted to focus on revenue-producing enterprises. That's when the funding decision began bouncing around to the two other entities involved.

Months went by without a decision being made, but Bob and his people began to sense that something wasn't right, not just with their group of investors but with the country at large. They noticed that many of the construction cranes that dotted the Dubai skyline were no longer operating 24/7. They heard rumors about financial concerns, about growing deficits, about suppliers who weren't getting paid. They heard a change of tone on the part of Dubai leaders—they no longer were as gung ho on spending whatever money was necessary to create a world-class company.

Eventually, Bob and his people got the message. The government and the investors wanted Bob to shut down the university without telling him to do so directly, and that's what he did since it was the only way to get out of that particular limbo.

The Leader-Limbo Factor

In a strange but very real way, limbo is a way to protect leaders from losing face. Two leaders we have dealt with extensively, the sheikh in Dubai and Lee Kuan Yew in

Singapore, were insulated from failure. Their staffs were fiercely protective of these powerful leaders' reputations, trumpeting their successes and blaming failures on others. Saving face is important in both countries, and the heads of these countries have a huge amount of face they must maintain. As a result, the leaders' inner circle goes to great and sometimes absurd (at least to Western minds) lengths to protect their face.

To save face, these leaders' staffs may take actions that put a wide variety of projects and programs in limbo. Rather than admit that an initiative launched by the sheikh or Lee Kuan failed to live up to expectations, these leaders' staffs simply put it permanently on the back burner. They keep salaried people in positions where they no longer are actually working toward goals but are simply shuffling papers. Rather than admit that an ambitious construction project lacks the funding to be completed or that an environmental initiative failed to reduce pollution, they maintain staff that was supposed to supervise these programs but is now supervising nothing substantive.

This commitment to protect leaders from losing face extends to the business community, and it sometimes results in actions that produce limbo. In developing countries, people in positions of responsibility are often more reluctant than their Western counterparts to move anything forward that comes with a significant risk of failure. As soon as they realize that this risk exists, they may quietly shut down an approved program or project. This is especially true of midlevel managers who are extremely concerned about face—not only their own but that of their boss and their boss's boss. They want to protect these senior executives from the embarrassment attached to a project that bombs in a highly visible manner.

Some companies and leaders in developing countries aren't subject to this generalization. They have been Westernized to the extent that they are even more willing to take risks than the typical Western entrepreneur. More to the point, they hate limbo as much as that action-oriented entrepreneur. Therefore, you need to assess how your boss, CEO, and other senior leaders from your developing country relish or reject limbo. To that end, ask the following questions:

- Have you witnessed them being reluctant to accept responsibility when something goes wrong or a mistake is made?
- Are people in your organization quick to cover up the mistakes of others one level above them?
- Have you noticed that leaders tend to avoid any projects that carry risk that is above the norm?
- Does the head of the country in which you're working routinely take credit for successful ventures and avoid any hint of blame for any of the failures?
- Does your boss usually articulate his enthusiasm for projects with low levels of risk and reward but seems far less enthusiastic for those carrying a moderate risk level and potentially a high reward?

If the answer to most of these questions is yes, then you need to be aware that sooner or later, you're likely to find something you're working on stuck in limbo. Fortunately, strategies exist to get out of this frustrating, unproductive state.

Strategies for Leaving Limbo

Admittedly, limbo can be complex and confusing. Talk to a number of people who have been leaders and managers in developing countries, and they'll describe bureaucratic quagmires that left them tearing out their hair in frustration. They'll relate stories of being caught in a no-man's-land between approval and implementation, and they'll complain about being trapped in mazes reminding them of *Alice in Wonderland* and where it seemed as if there was no way to reach their goal in the complex and confusing environment in which they were operating.

Limbo is particularly vexing to the Western mind, but people in developing countries are much better equipped to handle this state. They don't become nonplussed by limbo the way we do. Instead, they accept that periods of inactivity will occur, and that more likely than not, opportunities will arise to emerge from this inactivity and resume implementing a plan or strategy. We suggest adopting this calm, watchful attitude and waiting for your chance to use one or more of the following tactics to extricate your project or concept from limbo.

- Leverage the why behind the limbo.

If you can figure out why things have stalled, then you may have the knowledge necessary to know what to do next. In some instances, limbo in developing countries is caused by fixable factors. A project is stalled because you unknowingly offended a senior leader with an offhand comment you made; he's holding up your project until you apologize. Thus, a simple apology will get you out of limbo.

Most of the time, though, it's not that simple. But if you start talking to people and investigating the cause—and if you can get past all the evasive talk and the excuses and the "I don't knows"—someone may actually give you a hint about what's really going on. Be persistent. Play detective and ask probing questions. Insist to your people that you want them to be honest and that you won't hold what they tell you against them. You may discover that powerful interests in the government or elsewhere have put a hold on your strategy for their own reasons. You may find that the company's CEO is battling other factions in the company that are pressuring him to give their projects priority over yours. Sometimes, this knowledge can help you find a way to extricate yourself from limbo. At other times, it may not get you out of limbo but at least prevent you from wasting any more time on a program that isn't going anywhere in the near future.

- Adopt a nudging strategy.

Depending on what you discover using the previous tactic, you may find that a nudging strategy provides a way out of limbo. Nudging works best when the delay is bureaucratic red tape or a delicate situation. In the latter case, it may be that someone stands to lose face if your project moves forward—maybe someone else in the company will feel slighted. In the former case, it's possible that your proposal or idea has become stuck in the slow-moving implementation mechanisms that often characterize companies in developing countries. To a certain extent, these companies possess similar processes and procedures as big corporations in the United States had in the 1950s and 1960s. A series of individuals have to sign off before a project is funded and launched; a great deal of paperwork has to be completed before anything actually happens. You may not be aware of all the approvals and paperwork required, and from your perspective the stall may seem inexplicable.

A nudging strategy is nothing more than a way of gently pushing a project forward through consistent questioning and other nuanced methods. For instance, you should regularly ask your boss what's happening with a given project or e-mail a series of suggestions to bosses proposing alternative ways of moving something forward (for example, with a smaller budget than originally proposed). Or you could schedule meetings designed to revisit the idea or program in limbo and have an open discussion about the issues involved or have a private conversation with a senior leader who might be able to use his influence to cut through the red tape or handle the delicate situation.

- Throw a "soft" fit.

This doesn't mean throwing a hissy fit or some other insulting temper tantrum that makes you look like the stereotypical Ugly American or Ugly European. As we've emphasized, natives of developing countries tend to view Western managers who lose their cool as weak. Whether you're browbeating a direct report or becoming upset in front of your boss, you lose stature within the organization as result.

A soft fit, on the other hand, is something that your colleagues and bosses will understand and accept. To make your point, you're forceful without being overly emotional and insistent without being strident. Sometimes you need to let people know you mean business, that you're upset about being in limbo, and that it's hurting the organization to remain in this state.

In Dubai, Bob realized that one of his initiatives was languishing in limbo, and he investigated the matter and was told that the sheikh had rejected it. This news surprised Bob, who was sure that the sheikh had originally voiced his support of the initiative. Bob sent what he terms a "carefully worded text" to the sheikh explaining that he was told that the sheikh had put his program on hold and requested a meeting to discuss the matter and understand his concerns. Almost immediately, Bob received a return text message from the sheikh saying that no one had ever approached him about this initiative since he and Bob had talked about it months earlier. The sheikh quickly assembled the appropriate people in a room, expressed his desire that the initiative move forward, and it immediately emerged from limbo.

- Be persistently patient.

In some cases, you have to wait out limbo. For reasons you can't figure out—and may never figure out—your project has unofficially been put on hold. We've talked about the value of patience, and it can serve you well in limbo. Jeannie, an executive who worked for a US company in India, told us that her boss, an Indian male at least ten years her senior, approved a pet project she presented to him but then failed to provide her with the resources necessary to work on the project—she needed a travel allowance to study the best practices at retail establishments in different parts of India as well as two researchers to assist her. When she asked when these resources would be forthcoming, her boss would smile and say "soon" or words to that effect. Two months passed, and soon had still not arrived. Jeannie had just about had it when she talked to a colleague who was back in the United States but had previously worked for this same boss. He told her that this Indian manager liked to provide his people with a number of odd "tests" but he never informed his direct reports that they were being tested. This colleague told Jeannie that he suspected this was one of these tests.

With this knowledge, Jeannie resisted her impulse to demand the promised resources or to ignore the promise entirely. Instead, she instinctively recognized that her boss would respect her persistence as long as it wasn't accompanied by criticism or complaining. Sure enough, one month later he provided her with the resources he had committed to give her.

Persistent patience is a good tactic if you can distinguish whether your limbo is a long no or a slow yes. Because Jeannie's colleague told her he suspected her boss was testing her, she assumed that her limbo was a slow yes. You need to acquire the information that will help you understand if you're dealing with a no or a yes. The odds are that if you receive a lot of "I don't knows" in response to your questions, the issue becomes an undiscussable, and you're lied to, then it's probably a long no. If, on the other hand, your boss and other senior leaders are open with you about the reasons for the delay, or you identify a logic that explains the limbo you're in and suggests it's temporary, then persistent patience might help you emerge from the drift you've been in.

- Issue an ultimatum.

This is more of a last resort to get out of limbo, but it may work if you have sufficient clout with your boss or provide great value to the organization. Essentially, this tactic involves communicating, "Get me out of limbo—or else!" Be aware that this is a last resort because it could be the last thing you do for the company—your ultimatum may get you fired or force you to quit. Still, if issued at the right time by the right person in the right way, it can jar senior managers, a board, or other influential parties in a way that the other tactics cannot.

The right person aspect of the ultimatum just means that you must have sufficient stature within the organization so that your ultimatum carries some weight. The right way means that you make your demands without causing anyone else to lose face (for example, blaming someone as part of the demand). The right time means being aware of deadlines and other time-sensitive issues that will cause your ultimatum to gain force—for example, you issue your ultimatum at a time when the organization is increasingly dependent on you because of its entry into an area where you're the company's top expert.

Again, ultimatums should be used judiciously, but if nothing else can get you out of limbo, this tactic may help restart your stalled project.

When You Cannot Extricate Yourself

While we've found that in most cases the limbo state is not permanent, we should warn you that sometimes it is. In these instances, it's the wise Western manager who recognizes that limbo is going to stretch on indefinitely and that it's best to call a halt to whatever project has been stalled and move on to something else. We realize that this isn't a good situation, considering all the time and energy you have invested in a given initiative—for example, Bob hated to shut down the successful university that was crucial to DAE's strategy. But it's better to acknowledge limbo and leave it behind for another venture than to remain in it for additional weeks or months.

How do you know when you should call it quits rather than try to use the tactics we've delineated to pull yourself out of this state? Most obviously, when you've already tried some of these tactics and gotten nowhere, then that's a signal that you should change tactics—move on to another project or work task.

But as a general rule, close the books on a project when two of the signs we discussed earlier appear in tandem: a big gap between approval and action and your project becoming an undiscussable. Or, put another way, time plus silence indicates a deeply entrenched limbo. It may be that at some point in the future, you can revive the task or idea you were pursuing, but for now take a cue from your native colleagues and accept that some things aren't meant to happen. Call it a Zen philosophy or a real-world, mind-set for the developing world, but it will serve you well on those occasions when you're locked in limbo.

Learning from Limbo

Limbo provides Western leaders with insights into their developing countries—insights that can easily be missed due to the frustrating aspects of sustained inaction. Rather than stew and complain when nothing is happening, try to figure out what this tells you about the business environment in which you're operating. You may learn, for instance, that whenever you present a plan to change the company's outmoded software system, you encounter polite and sustained resistance. People keep telling you that your plan makes perfect sense, but they never act on it.

What does that tell you? It may mean that the software system is an untouchable; the person responsible for it may be the CEO or some other powerful individual in the company, and no one wants to insult him by acting on the plan. Or it may mean that the way you presented it created the limbo—though you didn't intend to insult anyone with your presentation, something about your manner or what you said had this effect.

Western leaders in developing countries often say that they can't figure out their new company or country. Limbo is an opportunity to start figuring them out. Contrary to what you may believe, it's not that things are completely illogical or random in the country. It's that you haven't yet figured out the logic that explains them. The strategies for leaving limbo we presented earlier may not always be effective, but as you put them into practice, they will probably give you some insights into the culture and the thinking that caused your initiative to become stuck. Obviously, you want it to become unstuck, but even if that doesn't happen, you can use the experience to obtain the unvarnished truth about how things work rather than settling for the edited or inaccurate version told to all Western leaders.

CHAPTER 9

Refine Your Instincts before Relying on Them

Just about every manager in a developing country we spoke to related a story with the following moral: Sometimes you've just got to trust your gut. Their stories all revolved around situations that were foreign to them. They found themselves having to make decisions without having access to sufficient information; or they were dealing with bosses who seemed to be motivated by currying favor with influential people rather than by achieving business goals; or they struggled to understand directives they were given or found themselves dealing with contradictory objectives.

Logical analysis didn't tell them what to do. Neither did falling back on what they had been taught in school or on the job. Nothing had prepared them for the choices or situations they faced, and there was no way to know how to respond in these instances. What was particularly troubling to some of these managers was that a lot was riding on what they did—the outcome of a project, the financial well-being of their division or company, and their own career success. While they had faced difficult choices as managers and leaders in the West, at least there they had felt they understood what each choice entailed and could use logic and experience to increase the odds of making the right one. Without the ability to rely on logic and experience, the only other option was to trust their gut.

Interestingly, though, many of these managers found their gut was a much more reliable guide after they had been in their new country for a period of time. To understand how this is so and how you can use this inner resource in challenging situations, we first need to define what it is.

An Inner Compass

"Gut" has a number of synonyms: "instinct," "intuition," "sixth sense," "hunch," and so on. It's that inner compass that provides direction when you feel lost, that helps you know when to take a risk and when to play it safe, that pushes you in a direction you might not ordinarily take. In the West, you may not need this inner compass much, since you can reason out the right direction based on familiar circumstances. The more volatile, strange, and ambiguous your circumstances, however, the more you need to rely on your instincts rather than your reason.

The problem, of course, is that your instincts have been shaped by your Western experiences, and they may inadvertently steer you off course. For instance, in Dubai Bob had two members of his team, a human resources executive from Pakistan and a strategy executive from Iran, who despised each other. It wasn't a personality clash like you might find in the West but the result of cultural and religious differences. Bob knew how to handle personality conflicts and other work tensions between individuals from his many years as an executive in the West, but because the issues between these two people were rooted in culture and religion, Bob wasn't quite sure what to do. He decided to rely on his gut and do what he would have done in the West: put the two individuals in a room and work with them to iron out their differences.

It was a disaster. As Bob noted at the time, it was like pouring kerosene on a fire. As he talked to them trying to understand each point of view, rather than facilitating a mutual understanding, he ended up ratcheting up the tension between them to an even higher level. While Bob kept waiting for them to apologize and compromise, they dug their heels in more firmly and with greater hostility.

Similarly, Karen was the head of a sales team in Asia, and she was attempting to close a deal with a new customer. It seemed clear to Karen that they had a deal in everything but ink—they had agreed on all the particulars, and she and the head of the customer team seemed to get along well. All that was left was for him to sign the contract. Yet he told Karen that he wasn't quite ready to do so, suggesting that he needed more time to study the deal. This made Karen anxious. In similar situations with her former employer in the West, when prospective customers said they needed more time to study the deal, it meant they were listening to other pitches from competitors. Karen's instinct told her that if she was going to make this deal happen, she needed to act fast. She e-mailed her counterpart in the customer organization that she was willing to cut their product price by 5 percent if that would clinch the deal and allow them to move forward.

Karen was surprised to receive an angry phone call from this customer, saying that he didn't appreciate that she was being so pushy and that the original price was fair and acceptable. Karen apologized profusely though she wasn't sure what exactly she was apologizing for. Fortunately, the deal went ahead, but she began asking colleagues what she had done wrong. When she described the situation, they told her that it was common for weeks to elapse between settling on terms with a customer and signing the contract and that in their culture rushing into a deal was considered bad form and that "studying it" was really a code phrase for providing a cognitive transition to a new supplier for everyone in the customer's company.

We're not suggesting here that you should ignore the instincts you developed in the West but rather that you refine them based on careful observations and firsthand experience in your new country. Let's look at some ways you can put this refinement process into action.

Tailoring Your Instincts to Your Culture

Given sufficient time and exposure to any foreign culture, most managers adapt. Over a period of months or years, most people working in developing countries hone their instincts so that even in confusing situations they can sense what the right thing to do is. Most of you, though, probably don't have months or years. Whether you're expected to hit the ground running or to get up to speed after a relatively short break-in period, you need to start using the right instincts relatively quickly. The following suggestions, therefore, are ways to accelerate the process of honing your instincts to the situations at hand:

- Pay close attention to anomalous behaviors.

Invariably, you'll notice that your colleagues say or do things that thwart your expectations of how people should act. Don't just disregard these anomalous occurrences. Don't just shake your head and decide that it's impossible to understand certain things in this country. Instead, view anomalies as treasure troves of knowledge about your developing country.

For instance, observe direct reports and bosses for actions that seem to deviate from the norm. When Bob was working in Singapore, he noticed that his people refused to volunteer their ideas during meetings. They would respond quickly and intelligently to questions and were fine with factual reports, but when Bob would request that they provide their own perspectives and suggestions, they'd clam up. This was an anomaly since everything in his experience as a manager told him that direct reports relish the opportunity to express their opinions and show their creativity. Over time, Bob resisted his Western instinct to ask directly that they provide their ideas and instead was more indirect in his approach; he found that they were much more willing to provide their ideas one-on-one and after they had gotten to know him better.

Similarly, pay attention to bosses who give you tasks or provide direction that strikes you as unusual or odd. One manager in a developing country told us that when he worked in a small Asian country, he had a boss who was elaborately courteous to him. When his boss gave him an assignment, it was always framed as a request. If his boss had something negative to say, he would couch it in the mildest terms possible, being sure not to give offense. Over time, this manager noticed that his boss's behavior was reflective of the extreme courtesy practiced by executives in the company, and he learned to read the nuances of this courtesy—a short, polite thank you might indicate dissatisfaction, for instance. By paying close attention to these nuances, this manager refined his instinct about the messages that were being communicated.

- Be attuned to the culture's implementation pace and work style.

How much (or little) time does it take to accomplish common work tasks? What are the hallmarks of a given business culture? In terms of the former, does it seem to take forever to implement a strategy, or are new policies rolled out at the drop of a hat, or is there an odd stop-and-start pattern to implementation? In terms of the latter, what is the most common form of communication—one-on-one or groups? Do people tend to work similar schedules as in the West or are time frames different? Are risk taking and creativity esteemed or eschewed?

The odds are, the pace and style of a developing country's business culture is different from the one you're used to. Too often, Western managers thrust into these cultures resist the pace and style rather than get in sync with it. They complain about how slow things go, for instance, or they attempt to impose the pace and style they're accustomed to on their work group. This response is counterproductive for a number of reasons, but the main one is that it prevents you from refining your instincts.

Try to get a feel for the distinctive traits of your culture. Be open-minded about it rather than judgmental. Approach it as a learning experience rather than a frustrating task. In this way, you'll gain an appreciation for the particular way work is accomplished in your country and company, and this will sharpen your instincts to the point that you can rely on them.

- Monitor the outside (of your company) environment for distinctive traits and changes.

Most of you will make some attempt to gain familiarity with your new country, usually both before you get there and right after you arrive. Typically, these actions involve learning the language at a rudimentary level, becoming familiar with the country's history, visiting local markets and monuments, and so on. This is great, but too often the learning stops shortly after you start the job. In many instances, you become so enmeshed in your daily responsibilities and challenges that you lose touch with everything that is happening outside of the office (unless you have a position that demands involvement with the community and government, such as being the country head of office).

What we're recommending here is making a regular effort to observe the country's politics, culture, religion, and economy. You can do this in a number of ways, but the easiest is probably reading local newspapers, either in hard copy or online. Engage in discussions about local politics and customs with native employees. Make an effort to see plays and concerts. Be especially watchful for distinctive characteristics of the country—characteristics that may be very different from the hallmark traits of Western environments. For instance, in one Indian community, a Western manager noted a far more communal atmosphere than in the city in the United States where he grew up. When he spent a day with a colleague and his family, people were dropping by constantly, and they visited two other households. Everyone was not only welcome but expected to visit. The notion of needing time alone struck this executive's hosts as sad and lonely.

Being aware of changes in this outside world, too, can be instructive. In Dubai, Bob noticed a number of unusual changes, including realizing that the cranes that dotted the skyline were no longer active 24/7 and that in the upscale high-rise condo where he lived, he seemed to be the sole occupant—all the other apartments were dark. It helped him develop his sense of the economics of Dubai and, by extension, his company. He no longer was naively operating based on his Western instincts but had refined them based on his awareness of environmental changes.

An Alternative Three-Step Process

Pak Chin, a vice president for a Fortune 100 aerospace company who is currently based in China and is Bob's close friend, has worked throughout Asia and has developed a process that has been highly effective in developing executive talent in Asian countries. In the previous section, we focused on how leaders can become attuned to the cultures of countries in which they're working, and Pak Chin's process offers another approach to accomplish this objective. Though he's used this process in Asia, we believe it's transferable to any developing country. In fact, it's especially useful for leaders who need to grasp the nuances and motivations of employees in their particular country.

The first step in Pak Chin's process is familiarization. As the word suggests, this step involves bringing an open mind and willingness to learn to a new culture in order to understand the politics, the economic forces, and all the other cultural issues. But the real goal beneath this understanding is, in Pak Chin's words, "understanding why people act the way they do."

As an example Pak cites the need to understand why people in China are so competitive. By making an effort to investigate the causes, you discover that "It's the allocation system. Millions of kids compete in national exams to get into local colleges. So from a very young age, they've been conditioned to view everyone else as competition and to gain as much as they can for themselves. The social and economic consequences of not getting into a good college can be devastating, to the point that parents will go to extreme lengths to perpetuate and promote an environment of hyper competitiveness."

The second step is self-conditioning and self-adjustment. In other words, you take what you learned in the first step and change the way you think about the way employees communicate and act. This means accepting them for who they are, not who you might want them to be. We've found that Western leaders impose their own values and expectations on direct reports in developing countries. They may not do this consciously, but it dulls their instincts rather than refines them. They don't have a sense of how to respond because they haven't adjusted their mind-set. As Pak told us, "We have our ways. They have their ways.. . . Their ways of communication may not be to our liking, but they are effective locally."

The third step is the operational phase. This is about executing your mission as a manager and as a leader. According the Pak, the key here is figuring out the motivations of your people. He cautioned that it's not always about money; some direct reports will want your friendship or approval while others will respond to an investment of your time (in coaching them, for instance). Based on what you learned in the first two steps, however, you should be better able to discern what motivates them, especially because this motivation may be specific to their country and culture and different from what you might find in the West.

Refining your instinct can be challenging, and this process gives you another tool to meet the challenge. Pak's approach can also help you remember that refining your instinct is a process. It takes time, knowledge, and effort. It requires you to shift your own ideas. And it demands that you try to get into the heads of colleagues so that you don't impose your preferences and perspectives on them. The benefit of all this is that you'll develop a sense of what to do in a variety of situations—situations that previously were either baffling or caused you to make mistakes. With a refined instinct, you're much more likely to make correct leadership decisions.

Learn from the Masters

It's likely that you work with or for a native of your new country who is brilliantly instinctive. In developing countries, leaders survive by their instincts rather than by following a manual of best practices. This is true of dictators, presidents, religious chiefs, tribal leaders, and others. Closer to home—or your new home away from home, at least—you're likely to find someone in your organization who relies on instinct to run his group. It may be the head of the company or someone down the line, but by paying attention to how he makes decisions, manages people, and performs other tasks by the seat of his pants, you can learn a lot.

We're not suggesting you forget everything you learned as a Western manager—state-of-the-art business practices can be used and adapted in many places throughout the world—but that you employ your refined instinct as a fallback position when standard practices don't work. You can model your instinctive managerial behaviors on this type of manager, adopting and adapting as you go along.

First, though, you need to identify someone as an instinctive manager. To do so, look for these traits:

- lack of a particular theory of the case or formal approach to deal with typical business situations,
- a knack for anticipating problems before they get out of control and responding to them quickly,
- relative ease with all the strange and volatile issues that crop up in developing countries,
- an ability to sense what each direct report needs from him and respond with that need in mind,
- a willingness to deviate from a given strategy or approach if it seems it's not working,
- seeming prescience to guess what's going to happen next, and

- a talent for survival, for knowing the move to make and when to make it in order to avoid a major career or business loss.

For instance, Luis worked for a large coffee exporter in South America, and he was constantly facing head-spinning crises. One day a pesticide that the company had relied on for years to protect the seed of the fruit that grows on coffee trees (the seeds are what we refer to as coffee beans) was banned by the government. A week later, the pickers went out on an informal strike, demanding a wage increase. Most vexing of all was Luis's boss, an often irrational, unpredictable man no one knew how to deal with—except Luis. While a boss like this wouldn't be tolerated in most Western companies, he was related to the owner of the company and so had a guaranteed job. Luis, more so than anyone else in the organization, was adept at reading his moods and responding in ways that didn't provoke his boss. Most of the time, Luis could read him with one look. Once, this boss was threatening to fire three employees because they had been a few hours late turning in a project. He was in the middle of ranting and raving and chewing out these employees when Luis came into the room, saw what was happening, and told his boss he had to tell him a joke. Astonishingly, his boss allowed him to tell it and somehow, it tamped down his rage; he stopped yelling at his people or threatening to fire them. How Luis did it, no one knew, but it was the same way he managed to grasp exactly what move to make right before a crisis exploded. It wasn't that he could always solve major problems, but that he had a sense of what to do to limit the damage or when to act quickly to deal with an issue before it exploded into a huge difficulty.

Luis, like many instinctive managers in developing countries, usually kept his cool. His emotions didn't get in the way of his instincts. Rather than becoming overly anxious or overly angry and letting these emotions lead his decision making, he was able to coolly assess a situation and allow his instincts to work their magic. It wasn't that he was always right. It was simply that he more than most managers knew what to do when no one else seemed to have a clue.

When to Use Your Refined Instincts

To a certain extent, you can't plan when you're going to deploy your instincts like you can plan using a more accessible skill. Yet if your experience goes according to form, you're going to find yourself in situations that are confusing, and your standard operating procedure fails to get the job done. At these times, you naturally rely on your sense of the situations, your feel for what the right course of action might be. If you've refined your instincts sufficiently through the methods previously discussed, then they will serve you well.

We've found that there are certain instances when they come in particularly handy in developing countries. While the following list is hardly complete, it provides you with some situational flags that might alert you to respond to a situation instinctively rather than based on conventional Western wisdom:

- When you are being pushed to do something you don't want to do.

Circumstances sometimes conspire to place managers in developing countries in difficult situations. It may be that a boss is insisting that you carry out a strategy that doesn't to work or that your team is urging you to take an action that may have negative consequences. Typically, people make good arguments for doing what they recommend, and part of you may think, "It's their country; maybe they know something I don't." And they might. On the other hand, your combination of Western experience and your growing knowledge of how things work in your new country may provide you with insights they lack.

For instance, we related a story earlier about when Bob was in Dubai and his advisors were urging him to go to the sheikh and accuse the individuals who were creating problems for the company. This was how things were handled there—people appealed to the highest power possible in (or outside of) an organization to fix a problem. Bob, though, instinctively recognized that complaining to the sheikh wasn't the answer. He sensed that he needed to develop a solution orientation among his people rather than a problem focus. He wanted to model behaviors for them to solve their own problems rather than running to an all-powerful figure to fix things. So he resisted the suggestions of his advisors, went with his own instinctive response, and helped his group deal effectively with this problem through their own efforts.

- When you need a plan B.

In other words, you try plan A, and it doesn't work even though you were sure it would be successful. You're faced with "Now what?" In developing countries, things often don't go according to plan. While things also go awry in the West, there is usually a logical fallback position—for example, when the product introduction is less successful than the company hoped, you study the numbers and analyze what went wrong before rolling it out again. In developing countries, however, that same product introduction may have been thwarted by civil unrest and looting of stores or by a company executive being put in jail for being a political dissident or because the factory has been seized by guerilla fighters or damaged by the monsoons.

Everything is thrown topsy-turvy, and it's at this point you have to come up with an alternative to save the day or get things moving again. This is where instinct is critical. The plan B that your instinct helps devise usually isn't the expected response to a failed plan A—it's improvised and probably not found in a business textbook. But you're sufficiently well-versed at this point in how things work in your company and country, and you take both environments into consideration as you concoct your plan B.

It may be something as simple as giving all your employees a day off even though pressure is building to meet an impending deadline and you haven't been making much progress. Or it may involve restructuring the company in an unorthodox manner, based on your sense that a hierarchical structure no longer suits the changing culture of the company or the country.

- When you're dealing with a problem or issue you've never dealt with before.

It's not just having to handle the impact of surprises, such as monsoons and civil unrest, on the business. You may have an employee who tells you he needs the next two weeks off to go on a pilgrimage, or you may discover that one group of employees is unable to work productively with another group because of religious or ethnic differences. No manual exists on how to manage in these circumstances.

Instead, you have to feel your way through the strangeness to arrive at effective approaches. Tony, for example, was working for a US company in China, and he and a number of other Western managers noticed that a drop in productivity at a company plant coincided with their arrival. No one could figure out what was wrong, and most of Tony's fellow managers determined that the productivity decrease was coincidental to their arrival. These Western managers had made an effort to get to know their people, had reassured them about their jobs, and had installed a new system for bonuses and raises tied to productivity.

Tony, more than his other managers, made an effort to get to know the people and culture of the country. When he wasn't working, he spent a lot of time visiting the homes of Chinese colleagues and attending various events in the nearby major city. Over time, he recognized that many Chinese people react negatively to arrogance and favorably to humility. Though he knew that he and his colleagues didn't think of themselves as arrogant, he also was aware that they spoke with great confidence of what they might accomplish and what they had accomplished in their previous assignments. Tony's instinct was that they should tone down their boasts about their successes and should make an effort to express their uncertainty when they were genuinely uncertain. Most of Tony's colleagues went along with his suggestion, and over time productivity began to climb to previous levels. While there was no way to prove that Tony's instinctive response was responsible, he and the other managers noticed that employees began to warm up to them in a way they had not in their first few months on the job.

The Advantages of Refined Instinct and Other Skills Learned in Developing Countries

Given the increased volatility and ambiguity in the most modern society as well as the most primitive, being able to operate effectively by the seat of your pants is becoming an essential managerial and leadership skill. Today far more than in the past, even CEOs of top companies must possess the capability to switch direction on a dime and be situational leaders. Even managers who are working in London, New York, and Tokyo are going to face dilemmas that their schooling and experience have not prepared them for.

Developing more effective instincts, therefore, will serve you well no matter what your position, company, or country. In a very real way, refining your instincts in a developing country prepares you to be a better manager and leader not just there but anywhere.

Throughout this book, we've discussed how you can be less frustrated and more effective when working in places like Dubai, Shanghai, Mumbai, and elsewhere. But applying the lessons found in these pages will be beneficial in many other ways. In a very real sense, an assignment in a developing country is a business training ground, one that not only helps you to be a better global executive but to experience growth as a leader.

Think about the principles discussed in each chapter. In the coming years, you're going to need to become adept at managing groups where the human capital maturity curve is more diverse than in the past. You're going to need to be far more flexible in the way you deal with programs, people, and policies than in the past. You're going to have to learn to

speak softer and listen harder in order to motivate and communicate with a mix of direct reports.

All this is happening because the global marketplace con-
tinues to evolve. You may work in the United States, but you
may find yourself managing a virtual team in New Delhi.
You may be working in an ultramodern office in Geneva, but
half your direct reports grew up in developing countries.

So the benefits of adopting the principles and mastering
the skills we've detailed are multifaceted. That's the long-
term view. In the short term, though, many of you are
embarking on assignments in countries that strike you as
exotic and where the ways of doing business seem illogical
or at least strange. You're managing people you can't quite
seem to understand even if you understand the language they
speak. You're dealing with biases and beliefs that are thousands of years old and that directly or indirectly affect how
employees carry out tasks. You're trying to get something
done today in a culture that is accustomed to getting things
done tomorrow.

We've been there. We and the people we interviewed have
found ways of meeting the challenges of leading and managing in developing countries, and we hope that what we've
learned will benefit you as much as it has benefited us.

INDEX